D0413908

How to Use, Adapt and Design

Knitting Patterns

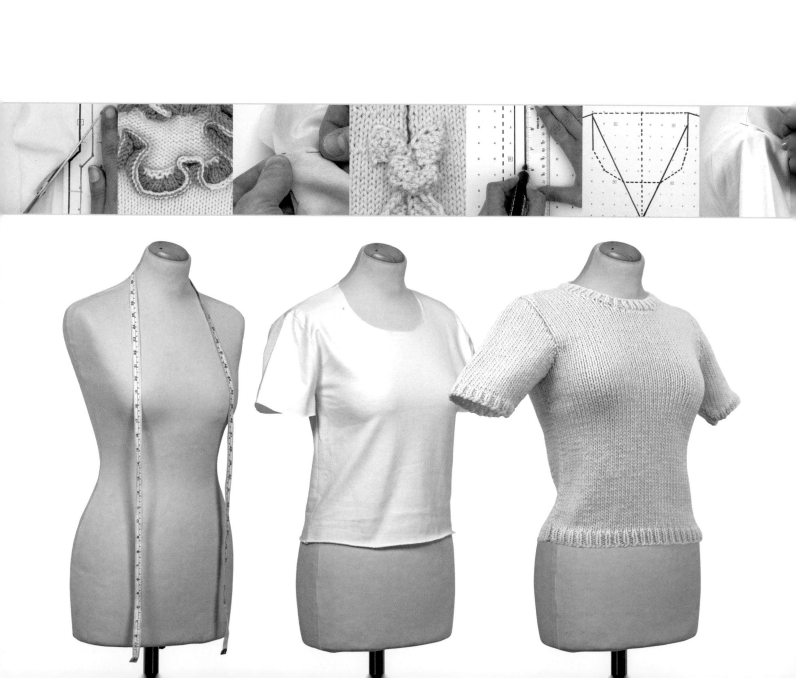

How to Use, Adapt and Design
Knitting Patterns

Sam Elliott and Sidney Bryan

Published in 2010 by
A&C Black Publishers
36 Soho Square
London W1D 3QY
www.acblack.com

ISBN 978-1-408-12761-2

Copyright © 2010 Quarto plc

All rights reserved. No part of this publication may
be reproduced in any form or by any means –
graphic, electronic or mechanical, including
photocopying, recording, taping, information
storage and retrieval systems – without the prior
permission in writing of the publisher.

A CIP record for this book is available from the
British Library.

QUAR.KNP

Conceived, designed and produced by:
Quarto Publishing plc
The Old Brewery
6 Blundell Street
London N7 9BH

Senior editor: Lindsay Kaubi
Technical editor: Betty Barnden
Copy editor: Claire Waite Brown
Art editor and designer: Julie Francis
Art director: Caroline Guest
Design assistant: Saffron Stocker
Photographer: Philip Wilkins
Illustrators: Kuo Kang Chen and
Terry Evans
Picture researcher: Sarah Bell
Creative director: Moira Clinch
Publisher: Paul Carslake

Colour separation in Singapore by PICA
Digital Pte Ltd
Printed in Singapore by Star Standard
Industries (PTE) Ltd

10 9 8 7 6 5 4 3 2 1

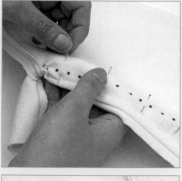

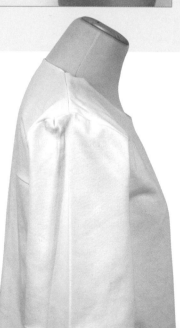
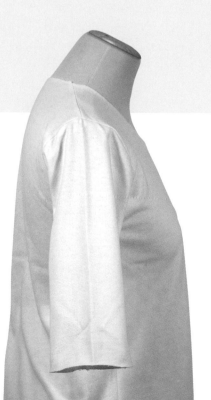
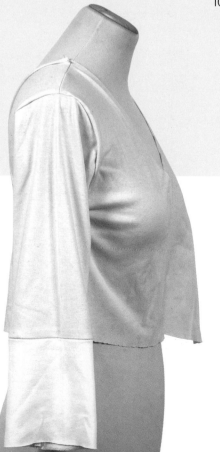

Contents

Introduction

Sid and I have been knitting both individually and as a team for the last 14 years; knitting is a passion that has grown alongside our friendship. We met at university and we both chose to specialize in constructed textile design, otherwise known as knitting. After graduation Sid continued his studies at the Royal College of Art in London and I started a design business selling knitted fashion swatches in Europe, Japan and the USA. Our careers have developed in different ways, teaching at highly regarded English universities, and working with some of the most compelling contemporary fashion designers currently practising. Through the years we have continued to share a design studio, and a love for progressive knitwear. We now work together on creative design projects, alongside Sid's successful menswear line.

Through discussion and practice we identified a real need for a knitting book that included techniques and methods to assist and support design and creativity in knitwear, enabling the reader to use, adapt and design their own knitting patterns. It was important to us that the book be written in a language that could be easily understood, allowing the reader to familiarize him or herself with the 'code' that is embedded in the world of knitting books.

The book combines both knitting and dressmaking methods in a practical and efficient way to inform and develop the skills needed to design an original knitted garment. The reader is guided through the process of creating and fitting a toile, a method that is frequently used in dressmaking but often overlooked by knitters. The benefits of creating a toile are that elements of the design can be checked before time is spent on writing a pattern and knitting large pieces, alleviating a disappointing outcome relating to fit or style and wasted expense. Designs are often changed at toile stage, because we're able to consider how the knitted fabric, choice of yarn and stitch will complement the silhouette. The extra time spent at the planning stages helps to ensure a successful and considered garment.

The reader is introduced methodically to the processes involved in using, adapting and designing a knitted garment from scratch. Useful tools such as charts and blank patterns that the reader can use to develop original knitting patterns support each process. The text is illustrated with step-by-step photography to make the techniques clear, and handy hints relating to each section help readers as they work through the design process and pattern-writing process.

Throughout the book, creative knitwear designed and made by Sid and me has been photographed and included, demonstrating the enormous range of possibilities of knitwear design, with the hope that this will inspire readers to create their own unique designs with confidence.

Sam & Sid

About this book

Design your own knitting pattern from scratch or adapt an existing pattern to get exactly what you want.

This book guides you through the process of buying and using commercial knitting patterns and then goes on to explain how to make your own knitting pattern from scratch. You'll learn how to adapt a pattern, whether it be the sleeves, neckline or body shape, and you'll discover how you can embellish your knitted pieces using stitch patterns, trims, embroidery and more.

Using knitting patterns (10–27)

This section of the book is a guide to using commercial knitting patterns, discussing everything from where to buy a pattern, right down to how to create and use a tension swatch. You'll also find out about reading knitting patterns, abbreviations and taking your own body measurements.

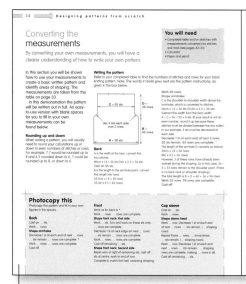

Designing patterns from scratch (28–61)

In this part of the book you will be taken step by step through the process of using an existing garment to create a knitting pattern. You will discover how to take initial measurements; convert measurements into stitches and rows; make a toile prototype; make alterations; write the pattern; and finally, assemble the garment.

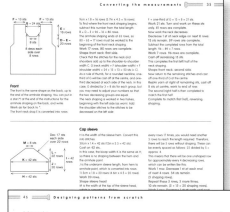

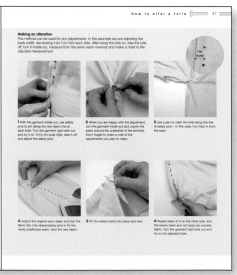

CHANGING SLEEVES

Choosing a sleeve design for your garment can be as simple as changing the length, or as complex as changing the shape, length, width and the way it is attached to the body. Either way, it is important that it works with the rest of the garment, and suits the purpose of the piece you are making.

Design options: Sleeves

As well as their practical use, sleeves can add interest to a garment, so consider your options carefully.

Here is a variety of sleeve types that you may want to use when adapting your pattern. When making your choice, try to achieve a balance in your design. If you have a complicated neckline, use a simple sleeve, and when using a highly designed sleeve, pick a simple neckline. Aim to use elements that contrast and complement each other rather than fight for attention.

The designer of this catwalk piece has chosen to use an exaggerated hishon sleeve on this dramatic garment. The knitted fabric gathers elegantly at the wrist, and works well with the choice of lightweight yarn.

Choosing the right length

When adapting your pattern, you have access to a variety of sleeve lengths, including a very short cap sleeve; short sleeve; to the elbow; bracelet or full length. When making your choice, you should consider how and when the garment will be worn, and what yarn it will be knitted in. For instance, a cap sleeve would normally be knitted in a lightweight yarn.

Choosing the right shape

The overall silhouette (or shape) of the garment will be affected by the choice of sleeve. Consider not only the length, but also the sleeve cap and cuff. Possible sleeve shapes include set in, raglan, raglan with yoke, dropped shoulder; cap, bell, leg of mutton; puffed and batwing.

The shape of the sleeve is often determined by how the cuff is designed. Some possibilities for the cuff include rib, ruffle, turn up drawstring, elasticised, stitch detail or roll edge.

SEE ALSO
Design details: Sleeves
See pages 64–67 for knitted examples of various sleeve types.

How to adapt the pattern (62–105)

Learn to adapt patterns to suit your tastes and body shape. Patterns needn't be set in stone – this chapter will show you how you can easily adapt the toile, paper patterns and written patterns. These changes can be applied to any part of the garment, including necklines, shoulders, sleeves and body shapes.

Embellishments (106–119)

Learn how to embellish your garments using stitch patterns, embroidery, appliqué, trims and fastenings, pom-poms and fringes, and beads and sequins.

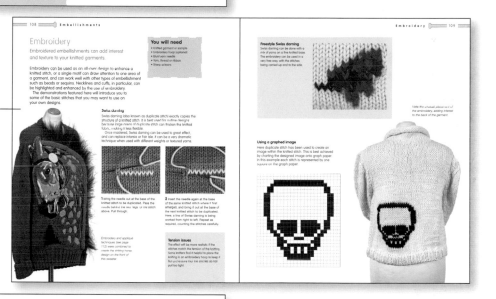

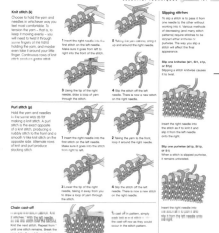

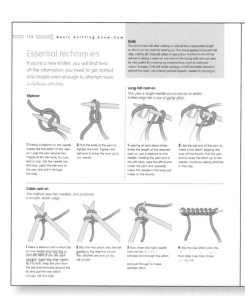

Basic knitting know-how (120–135)

Here you'll find a useful guide to all of the basic knitting tools and materials as well as a list of what you'll need to make a toile. There is also an indispensable refresher course on essential knitting techniques that serves not only as a great guide for beginners but also as a useful go to source for experienced knitters.

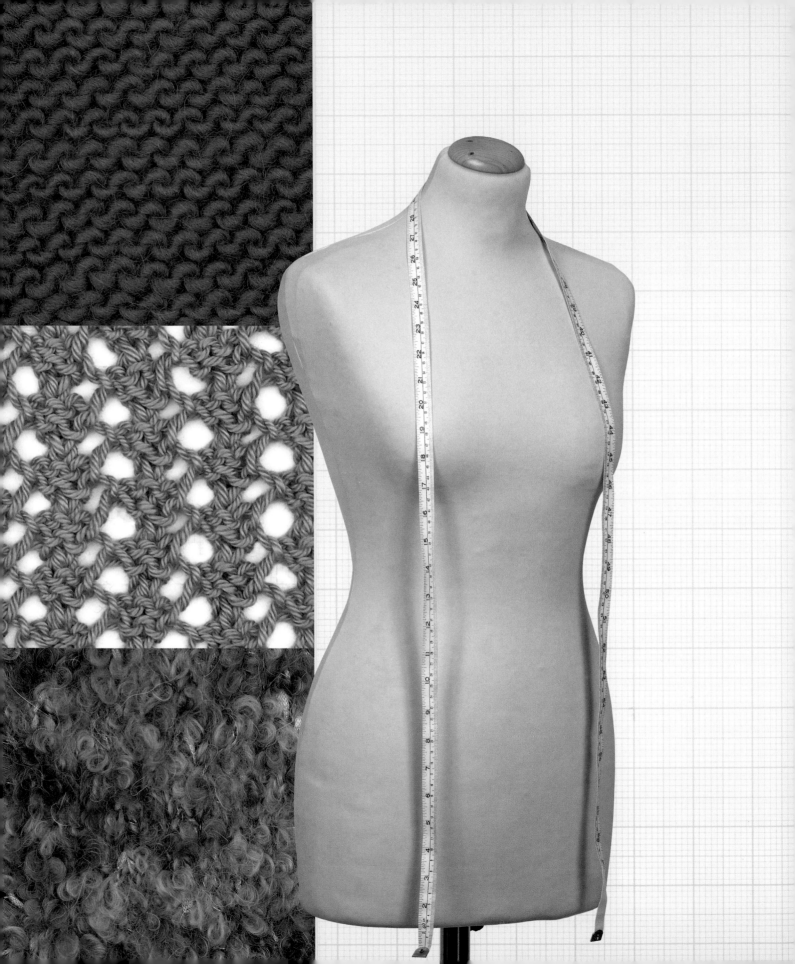

Part 1:
Using knitting patterns

This section aims to demystify all elements of the knitting pattern, and show how it can be used as a tool to help you create a perfect knitted garment. The chapter discusses ways to access knitting patterns – from blogs to shops – how to knit a tension swatch, and how to take your own body measurements. You will also find here a definition of pattern abbreviations and symbols. Once you have read this section, you will no longer be afraid of the knitting pattern, and will have a greater understanding of the elements involved in using one, enabling you to confidently tackle the next project of writing your own pattern.

ALL ABOUT KNITTING PATTERNS

Knitting patterns are available from a number of different sources, but all tend to use the same language. Here, we explain how to get hold of a pattern and what to do with it once you have it.

Sources of patterns

There are a variety of ways to obtain a knitting pattern.

With the rise in popularity of knitting, you can now find knitting patterns very easily. The most immediate source of information is online; however, if you prefer to have paper in your hands, there are lots of publications to help you.

There has also been a huge resurgence in the knitting circle, with knitting clubs and groups existing both globally and locally. To knit can now be a social experience, where you can meet fellow knitters and share information and techniques.

Online sources

There are a number of pattern sites that are easily accessible online. Knitting has become very social, and knitters are happy to blog and post feedback about patterns that they have completed, or swap hints on yarn. This information can be very helpful if you are experiencing problems, or in order to check patterns before you start a project.

Magazines

With the surge of interest in craft techniques has come a number of new magazines. Check women's magazines, fashion journals and specialized knitting magazines for free patterns and knitting projects; they can be great for getting ideas on new ways to use knitting.

Shops

Many craft shops are now developing their own lines of patterns and yarns. Specialist shops often have unusual custom yarns. Charity shops can be great for sourcing vintage patterns and books, needles and, if you are lucky, yarn. Vintage patterns knitted in modern types of yarn can look stunning, and you can reference old patterns and add your own details for a designer look.

Public libraries

Most libraries have a craft section with books containing patterns and projects.

SEE ALSO
Web resources
Find out about useful websites on page 137.

In recent years knitting groups have soared in popularity, making knitting a social event that can take place anywhere.

Anatomy of a knitting pattern

They come in many shapes and sizes... but there are lots of elements common to all knitting patterns.

Knitting instructions can seem daunting at first. However, once you're familiar with the conventions of abbreviations and charts, and understand the importance of correct tension (and how to obtain it), you'll be able to follow any pattern with confidence. The following information should help you understand the pattern better. Always read a pattern all the way through before you start.

Yarn and other materials

It is best to buy the exact yarn specified by the pattern, since any change in yarn will affect your tension and therefore the overall sizing of the garment – however, it is also possible to substitute a different yarn, as long as it is of the same weight. Always buy all the yarn required for your chosen size at the same time. Dye lots differ and subtle variations in colour can cause problems.

Tension (gauge)

This is the most important point on a pattern. Tension is a term that has been borrowed from the machine knitting industry, and which, in simple terms, means 'stitch size'. Tension, or 'gauge' can be changed depending on needle size and yarn weight – each hand-knitter will knit to an individual tension (how you hold the yarn makes the stitches tighter or looser), and therefore it is important that all pieces for a garment are knitted by the same person. Your tension must match exactly the tension given in the instructions; even a fraction of difference to the measurements will alter the size of your garment (see The importance of tension, page 18).

Finishing

'Blocking' is a knitting term for washing or steaming. It helps the stitches settle and creates a more even fabric. All yarn labels include washing instructions and you should consult the yarn label before blocking your finished pieces. Make sure you assemble the pieces in the order given in the knitting pattern. Instructions rarely give details of the type of seam(s) to use; for a selection of seams, see pages 61 and 135. It is important to take care at this stage; attention to detail is key to a high-quality garment.

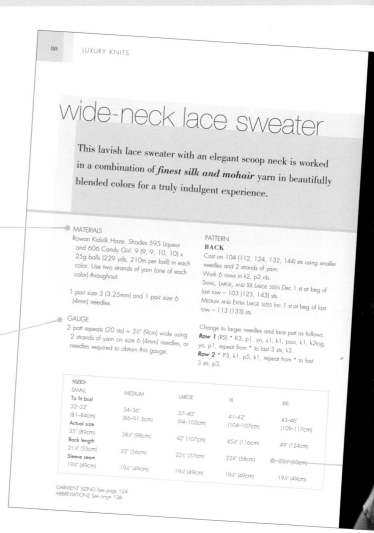

80   LUXURY KNITS

wide-neck lace sweater

This lavish lace sweater with an elegant scoop neck is worked in a combination of *finest silk and mohair* yarn in beautifully blended colors for a truly indulgent experience.

MATERIALS
Rowan Kidsilk Haze. Shades 595 Liqueur and 606 Candy Girl. 9 (9, 9, 10, 10) x 25g balls (229 yds, 210m per ball) in each color. Use two strands of yarn (one of each color) throughout.

1 pair size 3 (3.25mm) and 1 pair size 6 (4mm) needles.

GAUGE
2 patt repeats (20 sts) = 3½" (9cm) wide using 2 strands of yarn on size 6 (4mm) needles, or needles required to obtain this gauge.

PATTERN
BACK
Cast on 104 (112, 124, 132, 144) sts using smaller needles and 2 strands of yarn.
Work 6 rows in k2, p2 rib.
SMALL, LARGE, AND XX LARGE SIZES Dec 1 st at beg of last row – 103 (123, 143) sts.
MEDIUM AND EXTRA LARGE SIZES Inc 1 st at beg of last row – 113 (133) sts.

Change to larger needles and lace patt as follows.
Row 1 (RS) * K3, p1, yo, s1, k1, psso, k1, k2tog, yo, p1, repeat from * to last 3 sts, k3.
Row 2 * P3, k1, p5, k1, repeat from * to last 3 sts, p3.

SIZES				
SMALL	MEDIUM	LARGE	XL	XXL
To fit bust				
32–33"	34–36"	37–40"	41–42"	43–46"
(81–84cm)	(86–91.5cm)	(94–102cm)	(104–107cm)	(109–117cm)
Actual size				
35" (89cm)	38½" (98cm)	42" (107cm)	45½" (116cm)	49" (124cm)
Back length				
21½" (55cm)	22" (56cm)	22½" (57cm)	22½" (58cm)	23½" (60cm)
Sleeve seam				
19¼" (49cm)	19¼" (49cm)	19¼" (49cm)	19¼" (49cm)	19¼" (49cm)

GARMENT SIZING See page 124
ABBREVIATIONS See page 126

Abbreviations

Abbreviations are there to make your job easier. Most knitting patterns include a list of abbreviations. These will differ from one source to another: 'K1b', for example, may mean 'knit one in the back of the stitch' (through the back loop), or it may mean 'knit one in colour b' or even 'knit one in the row below'. Always read the abbreviations carefully and familiarize yourself with them. You may find it helpful to rewrite the pattern in your own way (see page 52). A list of common abbreviations is given on page 16.

Gr. M
ca. 350 g

Gr. 10J/A
ca. 250 g

4 – 5

Repeats

Two kinds of repeat are commonly used in knitting patterns:

Stitch repeats: These may be indicated by parentheses, for example '(K2, P1) 3 times' means knit 2 stitches, purl 1 stitch, knit 2 stitches, purl 1 stitch, knit 2 stitches, purl 1 stitch. Stitch repeats may also be indicated by asterisks, for example '* K2, P1, * repeat from * to * to last stitch, K1' means knit 2 stitches, purl 1 stitch, then repeat these 3 stitches over and over until you reach the last stitch of the row, knit 1 stitch.

Section repeats: Sometimes a whole section of instructions may be repeated – for example the instructions for a sweater front might read 'work as given for Back to **', meaning 'Follow the instructions for the back until you reach the symbol **', at which point you should return to the instructions for the Front to continue working. Sometimes sections are repeated several times.

WIDE-NECK LACE SWEATER   81

Row 3 * K3, p1, k1, yo, sl, k2tog, psso, yo, k1, p1, repeat from * to last 3 sts, k3.
Row 4 * P3, k1, p5, k1, repeat from * to last 3 sts, p3.
These 4 rows form lace patt repeat. Cont in patt until work measures 13⅜" (35cm).

Shape armhole
Bind off 3 (4, 5, 6, 7) sts at beg of next 2 rows.
Dec 1 st at each end of next and every other row until 91 (97, 103, 107, 111) sts remain. Cont without shaping until work measures 20½ (21, 21¼, 21½, 22)" [52 (53, 54, 55, 56)cm].

Shape neck
Row 1 Patt 29 (31, 33, 34, 35), bind off 33 (35, 37, 39, 41) sts, patt 29 (31, 33, 34, 35).
Work on these 29 (31, 33, 34, 35) sts for first side of neck.
Row 2 Patt.
Row 3 Bind off 5 sts, patt to end.
Rows 4–9 Repeat rows 2 and 3 three times – 9 (11, 13, 14, 15) sts.
Row 10 Patt.
Row 11 Bind off.

Second side of neck
Rejoin yarn to rem sts at neck edge and work rows 3 to 11 as given for first side of neck.

Shaping

Some instructions tell you in detail exactly how to work increasing and/or decreasing, whereas others may be more vague. For example, 'K2tog at beginning of every right-side row' (knit 2 together at beginning of every right-side row) tells you what decreasing method to use, whereas 'decrease 1 stitch at beginning of every right-side row' leaves the knitter to decide – in this case turn to page 130 to choose the best method.

Multiple sizes

If a pattern comes in different sizes, these will be set out in order from the smallest to the largest, either in a grid, or with the larger sizes in parentheses. Some patterns include measurements in both centimetres and inches: these two systems do not correspond exactly, so choose which system you want to follow and use it for the whole project.

Garment pieces

As a rule, it is best to work the pieces in the order given because there is probably a reason why they are in that order. For example, a pocket lining may need to be worked before knitting a front.

Schematics:
Some knitting patterns include schematics, which can be very helpful. Always check the measurement of each piece you knit against any measurements given.

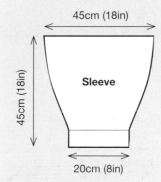

45cm (18in)

45cm (18in)

Sleeve

20cm (8in)

Sizing: Where different figures apply to different sizes, the figures for the larger sizes are usually given in parentheses. For example, 'cast on 48 (56, 64) stitches', means cast on 48 stitches for the small size, 56 stitches for the medium size and 64 stitches for the large size. To avoid mistakes, highlight the figures that apply to you. Where only one figure is given, this applies to all sizes.

SEE ALSO
Common abbreviations
Common abbreviations and symbols explained, see page 16.

The importance of tension
For a full explanation on the importance of tension and its uses in pattern writing, see page 18.

Constructing the garment
For finishing techniques and how to seam pattern pieces together, turn to page 58.

Common abbreviations

Always read the list of abbreviations used in any knitting pattern. Different suppliers may use different abbreviations, and they may be upper- or lowercase letters. Below are some of the most commonly used abbreviations.

alt	alternate	**Kwise**	knitwise	**rep**	repeat
approx	approximately	**LC**	left cross; left cable	**rev st st**	reverse stocking stitch
B	bobble or bead	**LH**	left hand		
BC	back cross; back cable	**lp(s)**	loop(s)	**RH**	right hand
beg	beginning	**LT**	left twist	**rib**	ribbing
bet	between	**M**	marker	**rd(s) or rnd(s)**	round(s)
BH	buttonhole	**m**	metre(s)	**RS**	right side (of work)
C	cable; cross	**MB**	make bobble	**RT**	right twist
CC	contrast colour	**MC**	main colour	**sk**	skip
col	colour	**meas**	measure(s)	**SKP, skpo**	slip 1, knit 1, pass slip stitch over
cm(s)	centimetre(s)	**mm**	millimetre(s)		
cn	cable needle	**m1**	make one	**sl**	slip
cont	continue	**m1tbl or m1b**	make one through back loop; invisible increase	**sl st**	slip stitch
dec(s)	decrease(s), decreasing			**sM**	slip marker
DK	double knitting			**ssk**	slip, slip, knit
dpn	double-pointed needle(s)	**ndl**	needle	**st(s)**	stitch(es)
EOR	every other row or round	**no**	number	**st st**	stocking stitch
ER	every row or round	**oz**	ounce	**tbl**	through back loop(s)
est	established	**P; p**	purl	**tog**	together
FC	front cross; front cable	**pat; patt**	pattern	**WS**	wrong side (of work)
foll	follow(ing)	**Pb; P1b**	purl stitch in row below; or purl stitch through back loop	**wyib**	with yarn in back, as if to knit
g, gr or gm	gramme				
g st	garter stitch			**wyif**	with yarn in front, as if to purl
in(s)	inch(es)	**Pbf**	purl into back and front of same stitch		
inc(s)	increase(s), increasing			**yb or ybk**	yarn to the back between needles
incl	include, including	**Pfb**	purl into front and back of same stitch		
K; k	knit			**yd**	yard
Kb; K1b	knit stitch in row below, or knit stitch through back loop	**pm**	place marker	**yf or yfwd**	yarn to the front between needles
		pnso	pass next stitch over		
		psso	pass slip stitch over	**yo or yon**	yarn over needle to make extra stitch
Kbf	knit into back and front of same stitch	**Ptbl**	purl through back loop		
		P2tog	purl 2 together	**yrn**	yarn round needle to make extra stitch
Kfb	knit into front and back of same stitch	**Pwise**	purlwise		
		RC	right cross; right cable		
K2tog	knit 2 together	**rem**	remaining		

Common symbols

Always read the list of symbols given in the key to any chart.
Patterns from different sources may use different symbols.
Some symbols are worked differently depending on whether
they fall on a right-side row (RS) or a wrong-side row (WS).

⊞	selvedge stitch
▯ or ▭	stocking stitch – RS: K, WS: P
▬ or •	reverse stocking stitch – RS: P, WS: K
℞ or ╱	twisted stocking stitch – RS: Ktbl; WS: Ptbl
V	slip stitch knitwise
V or ▯	slip stitch purlwise
O	yarn over
୪ or U	make one through back loop
┌ or V	increase 1 stitch – RS: knit into front and back of stitch; WS: purl into back and front of stitch
V	(k1, p1, k1) all in same stitch
V or ▼	multiple increase (refer to key)
◸ or ◿	right-slanting decrease – RS: K2tog; WS: P2tog
◺ or ◣	left-slanting decrease – RS: Skpo or Ssk; WS: P2tog tbl
◸ or ◢	right-slanting double decrease RS: K3tog; WS: P3tog

◥ or ◤	left-slanting double decrease – RS: sl1, K2tog, psso; WS: sl2tog, sl1k, sl 3 sts back to LH ndl and P3togtbl
∧ or ▲	multiple decrease (refer to key)
▬	cast off
■	no stitch
• or ◉	knot or bobble (refer to key)
⤬ or ⟋	right twist (2 sts)
⤬ or ⟍	left twist (2 sts)

larger twists and cables may be shown in various ways, eg:

⤬⤬ or ⟋⟋	cable 4 sts to right
⤬⤬⤬ or ⤬⤬	cable 6 sts to left

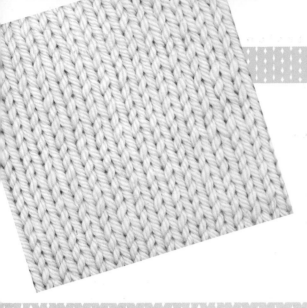

THE IMPORTANCE OF TENSION

Also known as 'gauge', tension describes the tightness of your knitting and is individual to you. Accurate tension allows an exact size of garment to be knitted. Each knitter works in a slightly different way, which is why you should check your own tension carefully.

Why make a tension swatch?

Making a tension swatch is highly recommended for a number of reasons.

A tension swatch provides the knitter with all the information needed to calculate the amount of stitches and rows required for a garment. The swatch can also be used to test how the yarn will look and feel, and to calculate how much yarn will be needed for a project.

Step-by-step sequences will show how to knit and measure a tension swatch correctly and illustrate how needle size and yarn weight can affect tension. It can be frustrating to knit a swatch when you want to get knitting, but your project will be better planned and more likely to fit if a tension swatch is first completed and used properly.

Patterns and ball bands

Most shop-bought patterns require you to complete a tension swatch, and you will later be shown how to use a tension swatch to develop your own patterns from scratch. The information on the ball band, or cone, will list the needle size to be used and tension to be achieved. The tension will be described by a number of stitches and rows to a certain measurement. Your tension swatch should match that given on the pattern.

If you knit loosely and your resulting swatch is larger, you will end up with larger pattern pieces; if you knit tightly, you will end up with smaller pattern pieces.

A chance to experiment

Making a tension swatch also provides a good opportunity to test colour combinations, stitch techniques and mixing of yarns. The absolute rule is that whatever you plan to do to your final garment should be done to your tension swatch. For example, if you plan to use a textured stitch on your garment, you must use the same stitch on your tension swatch.

1.75 oz · 50 g
110 yds · 102 m

55% Cotton • Coton
45% Nylon • Nylon

Purchase sufficient yarn of this dye lot as the next lot may differ slightly in shade.

Check your yarn ball band for information on yardage.

SEE ALSO
Making and measuring a tension swatch
Learn how to make and measure a tension swatch correctly on page 20.

How much yarn?

If you are working from a pattern book or leaflet:
- Consult the instructions and buy the correct amount for the required size of the exact yarn specified, making sure that all the dye-lot numbers match for each colour needed.
- If you want to make any pattern alteration involving extra knitting (such as longer sleeves), buy an extra ball or two.

To substitute a different yarn in a pattern book or leaflet:

- Find a substitute yarn that matches the original as closely as possible in yardage, fibre content and tension or see below.
- If the yardage does not match, calculate the total yardage of original yarn required. The quoted number of balls x original yardage = total yardage. Divide this number by the substitute yardage to find the number of substitute balls you need.
- If the fibre content does not match, consider whether the substitute yarn will drape in the same way as the original, and how it will feel in wear: For example, a summer top designed to be knitted in a silk or cotton yarn may be perfectly feasible in a substitute woollen yarn, but the result would be warmer to wear and springier, without the drape of a non-elastic yarn.
- If the tension does not match, you will need to make adjustments to the instructions to compensate. For a difference in row tension (measured lengthways), simply work more or fewer rows to match the measurements required for different parts of the design. However, if the stitch tension (measured widthways) does not match, this can be tricky, and another substitute should be considered. In either case, it is wise to buy an extra ball or two.
- Buy an extra ball anyway – you can always make a hat.

When designing or adapting patterns:

- If possible, consult existing pattern books/leaflets for the chosen yarn, to find a pattern similar to what you intend to design and make. Buy the specified amount of yarn, plus 10–15% extra.
- Another way is to buy just one ball and make a whole ball test piece: Using the needle size(s) you intend to use, cast on 50 stitches and work in the pattern you intend to use until the whole ball is used up. Make the sample representative of your project: if half the project will be in a textured stitch, or on smaller needles, make the sample the same way. Measure the test piece, for example, 25 x 30cm = 750cm square (10 x 12in = 120in square), then calculate the area of the pieces in your project, as shown at right.

Yardage

Yardage is the length of yarn contained in a ball, and may be (confusingly) given in metres. For example, 50g (2oz) of woollen DK yarn might contain 120m (130 yards), whereas 50g (2oz) of a cotton DK yarn, knitting to a similar tension, might only contain 98m (100 yards).

Calculating the area of the knitted pieces for your project

In this example, the back and front of the sweater are each 50 x 55cm = 2,750cm square (20 x 22in = 440in square); and the area of each sleeve is 45 x 32.5cm = 1,462cm square (18 x 13in =234in square).

The total area of the back, front and two sleeves = 2,750 + 2,750 + 1,462 + 1,462 = 8,424cm square (440 + 440 + 234 + 234in = 1,348in square). Add 15% extra to allow for inaccuracies in estimation and for details such as neckbands: 8,424 x 115% = 9,687cm square (1,348 x 115% = 1,550in square).

To find the number of balls required, divide this final total by the area of a whole ball test piece (see left). For example, 9,687 divided by 750 = 12.9 (1,550 divided by 120 = 12.9). So for our example, you would need to buy 13 balls of yarn. You may finish the project with yarn left over, but all knitters need a stash.

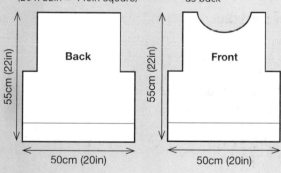

Approximate area:
50 x 55cm = 2,750cm square
(20 x 22in = 440in square)

Approximate area:
as back

Back — 55cm (22in) / 50cm (20in)

Front — 55cm (22in) / 50cm (20in)

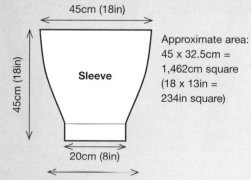

45cm (18in)

45cm (18in)

Sleeve

Approximate area:
45 x 32.5cm = 1,462cm square (18 x 13in = 234in square)

20cm (8in)

Average width:
45 + 20 divided by 2 = 32.5cm
(18 + 8 divided by 2 = 13in)

Making and measuring a tension swatch

How to knit and measure a tension swatch correctly.

Certain rules must be followed when knitting a tension swatch.

First rule: Use the yarn that you will use for the garment. Varying the yarn will change the measurements of the tension swatch and make any calculations incorrect.

Second rule: Knit the swatch in the same stitch that will be used for the garment. Varying the stitch will change the measurements of the swatch and make any calculations incorrect. Where several stitches will be used, knit your tension swatch in the main stitch to be used, or knit a swatch in each stitch to be included (see page 98).

Third rule: The swatch should be knitted by the person who will be knitting the garment. All knitters knit to their own personal tension. If a garment is being completed by more than one knitter, it is advisable for full sections to be completed individually.

Fourth rule: Treat the swatch in the same way you plan to treat the garment. For example, if the garment will be washed or ironed, do the same to the swatch. Some yarns – especially wools – react to washing and ironing and may shrink. Refer to the ball band for more information.

Big is better

As a general rule, the bigger the tension swatch, the more accurate it will be. As a guide, to get an accurate reading a tension swatch would normally be a square of 10cm (4in). Printed patterns sometimes suggest a tension swatch that is much smaller; however, it is preferable to work with larger swatches. Your yarn thickness will determine how many stitches and rows will be made in the swatch: A thick yarn will need fewer stitches and rows than a fine yarn.

You will need

- Yarn
- The right-sized knitting needles for your yarn
- Paper and pencil
- Ruler
- Pins
- Iron and ironing board
- Tape measure

Correct and incorrect tension examples

- It is important to keep an equal and correct tension when knitting to ensure you have equal and even-sized stitches. Here you can see the stitches are irregular (swatch on left).
- If you are knitting with too tight a tension, your knitting will have no stretch and will feel hard.
- If you are knitting with too loose a tension, your stitches will be sloppy and not hold their shape, and the resulting fabric will have little or no elasticity.
- Fabric knitted in the correct tension will spring gently back into shape, the stitches will look equal and consistent in size and the fabric should have a good handle and drape (swatch on right).

Incorrect tension swatch   *Correct tension swatch*

Measuring a tension swatch

It is important to get a correct measurement from your tension swatch, since these calculations will affect the size of your garment. For this exercise we have knitted a tension swatch using a chunky wool yarn. Following the instructions on the pattern or ball band, UK 6mm, US size 10 needles were used. 15 stitches were cast on, and 18 rows were worked.

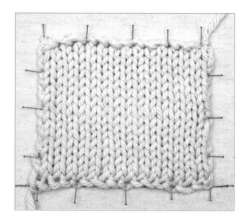

1 To measure your tension swatch, draw a straight line on either a sheet of paper or your ironing board. Pin the bottom of your swatch to the straight line, taking care not to distort the swatch. The swatch should lie as square as possible. Iron or steam the swatch if the yarn is suitable (see pages 58–59).

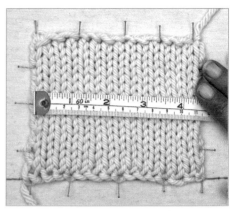

2 Lay a tape measure though the centre of the swatch, left to right and count the number of stitches in a 10cm (4in) length. The edge stitches may be distorted – take care to measure accurately. Here, there are 14 stitches to 10cm (4in).

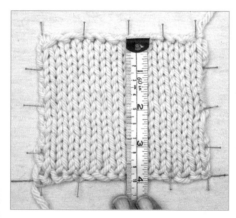

3 Lay your tape measure through the centre of the swatch from the top to the bottom and count the number of rows in a 10cm (4in) length. Again, the edge stitches may be distorted, so take care to measure accurately. Here the measurement is 18 rows to 10cm (4in).

Calculate your tension

Measure your tension swatch as shown above.

14 stitches equals 10cm (4in)
Divide 14 by 10 to give 1.4 stitches per cm.
Or divide 14 stitches by 4in = 3.5 stitches per inch.

18 rows equal 10cm (4in)
Divide 18 by 10 to give 1.8 rows per cm.
Or divide 18 rows by 4in = 4.5 rows per inch.

The tension swatch above gives a tension of 1.4 stitches and 1.8 rows per cm = 14 sts and 18 rows per 10cm (or 3.5 stitches and 4.5 rows per inch: 14 sts and 18 rows per 4in).

Matching the tension on a printed pattern

- If you have too many stitches or rows to 10cm (4in), your knitting is too tight, and you should make another swatch on larger needles, then remeasure as above.
- If you have too few stitches or rows to 10cm (4in), your knitting is too loose, and you should make another swatch on smaller needles, then remeasure as above.
- Continue making swatches on different needles until you are satisfied you have achieved the correct tension. Remember to make a note of the needle size you used.

SEE ALSO
Why make a tension swatch?
pages 18–19.
How needle size and yarn affect tension
pages 22–25.
Blocking and seaming
pages 58–61.

How needle size and yarn affect tension

Needle size and yarn weight can affect the size and look of a garment.

Most yarns come with a recommendation to use a certain needle size. If you knit with the recommended needle size and yarn, in theory you should find you are able to produce a tension swatch that meets the measurements stated on the pattern; however, in practice sometimes different knitters need different-sized needles to achieve the same tension with the same yarn. That's why a tension swatch is essential. If you want to substitute a different yarn in a pattern, it is best to find a yarn that is of the same weight and that uses the same needle size (see page 19).

When sourcing yarns be sure to consider how the knitted fabric will sit on the body: is it appropriate for your choice of garment?

Yarn weights

Before they can be used for knitting, most fibres need to be processed in order to form yarn. Each strand of fibre is known as a ply, and yarn is made up of a number of plies spun together.

The yarn produced can vary greatly in terms of thickness or weight. Traditionally, different terms are used to define different weights of yarn: for example, lace, four-ply, DK, Aran and chunky. The weights are approximations only, varying from one manufacturer to another. These yarns mainly come in the form of balls.

If you are using yarn on a cone, the yarn information should be inside the cone, and may feature a number such as 2/14. This means that two ends of yarn have been spun 14 times.

When using machine-weight yarns (coned yarns), hand-knitters often ply up the yarns themselves. This is easily achieved by winding off some of the yarn with a cone winder and knitting with more than one strand of yarn.

Fine yarn described as crochet thread, two-ply, three-ply or lace-weight is used to make delicate articles.

Four-ply or sock weight is fine to medium-weight yarn, often used for baby garments and other small projects.

Double knitting are medium-weight yarns with a wide range of uses. These popular weights are available in a huge choice of colours and fibres.

Aran-weight yarns are somewhat heavier than double knitting, suitable for many garments and accessories, and again available in a wide range of colours and fibres.

Chunky yarns are great for quick projects. This category has more variation than any other – some extra-thick yarns are described as extra-chunky or super-chunky.

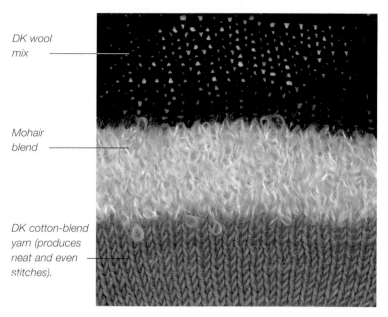

DK wool mix

Mohair blend

DK cotton-blend yarn (produces neat and even stitches).

Yarn weights and tension

You can achieve some interesting effects by varying the weight of the yarns you use within one garment, perhaps by changing to thicker needles and a chunkier yarn. Alternatively, try knitting pieces of the garment in different weight yarns, for example, chunky sleeves with a finer tension body.

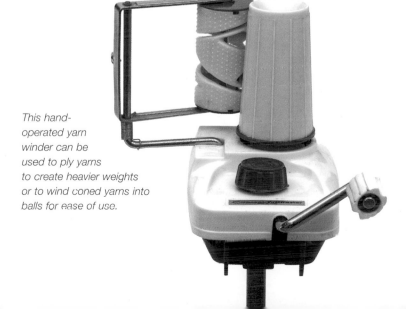

This hand-operated yarn winder can be used to ply yarns to create heavier weights or to wind coned yarns into balls for ease of use.

How needle size and yarn affect tension

Interesting effects can be achieved by knitting yarns on different-sized needles to those recommended, a technique called 'knitting out of tension'.

◄**1** Mohair yarn worked in stocking stitch (30 sts x 70 rows) has been knitted on the recommended needles (UK 4mm, US size 6), producing a neat and even fabric.

◄**2** The same mohair yarn as in example 1, knitted on larger needles (UK 6mm, US size 10) to create a more open, out-of-tension stitch (20 sts x 35 rows).

Continued ►

Tip

Label all your tension swatches with the yarn brand and needle size used, and details of any unusual stitch pattern. File them in a box, or glue them in a book (along with the ball bands), for future reference.

◀**3** Medium-weight woollen yarn, worked in stocking stitch (20 sts x 24 rows), using the needle size recommended on the ball band (UK 4mm, US size 6). This makes a fabric that is flexible, but firm enough to retain its shape when worn and washed.

▶**4** The same yarn as sample 3, with the same number of stitches and rows, but worked on larger needles (UK 5mm, US size 8). Each individual stitch is larger, so the whole sample is larger, and the fabric is looser, with more drape. It can be difficult to form even stitches with larger needles. Such knitting, using needles other than the recommended size, is called 'out of tension' knitting.

▲**5** Another example of 'out of tension' knitting, this time with smaller needles. The same yarn as sample 3, and the same stitches and rows, but worked on UK 3mm, US size 3 needles. This fabric is tighter and firmer than both samples 3 and 4, and the sample itself is smaller.

▲**6** Chunky (heavyweight) woollen yarn, with the same number of stitches and rows as samples 3, 4 and 5, worked in stocking stitch using the recommended needle size (UK 5mm, US size 8). The sample is about the same size as sample 4, but the fabric is firmer, with less drape.

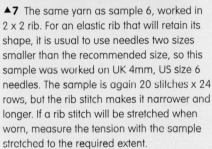

▲**7** The same yarn as sample 6, worked in 2 x 2 rib. For an elastic rib that will retain its shape, it is usual to use needles two sizes smaller than the recommended size, so this sample was worked on UK 4mm, US size 6 needles. The sample is again 20 stitches x 24 rows, but the rib stitch makes it narrower and longer. If a rib stitch will be stretched when worn, measure the tension with the sample stretched to the required extent.

◄**8** The same yarn and needles as sample 6, with the same number of stitches and rows, but worked in garter stitch (all rows knit). The stitch formation makes this sample a little wider than sample 6, and considerably shorter.

◄**9** Lightweight cotton yarn, with the same number of stitches and rows as samples 3–8, worked in stocking stitch using the recommended needle size of UK 3mm, US size 3. The sample is smaller than previous samples, but the flexibility and firmness are similar to samples 3 and 6.

◄**10** The same yarn as sample 9, worked on the same needles, with the same number of stitches and rows, but this time using a lace stitch. Although the sample is similar in length to sample 8, the looseness caused by the made stitches of the lace pattern makes the swatch wider.

◄**11** Some fancy yarns make it hard to distinguish individual stitches: Make sure you note down not only the needle size used, but also the number of stitches you cast on, and keep a record of the rows as you knit them, because you may find it difficult to count them later!

YOUR MEASUREMENTS

To make a perfectly fitting garment, it is vital that you accurately obtain the measurements of the intended wearer.

Collecting measurements

How to take measurements from the body.

There are two ways to collect your measurements. The first is to take your own measurements. The second method is to measure an already existing garment that fits you perfectly (see page 30). To take your own measurements, it is helpful to have an assistant, because bending your body to look down can alter your measurements. On the opposite page is an easy-to-use blank table for you to fill in your own measurements.

Getting started

Start by asking for help from a friend. It is virtually impossible to take accurate measurements by yourself. Use a dressmaker's measuring tape. Remove all of your outer clothing, but remain in your underwear while measuring. Use the standard size UK12/US8 measurements (shown opposite) to compare with your own. Use the diagrams provided opposite as a guide to where to take the measurements. These measurement points are called 'body landmarks'. Body landmarks can be indicated on your body by positioning sticky tape on your underwear. Fit the tape measure snugly around the widest part of the area being measured. Do not measure too tightly or too loosely.

Fit and actual measurements

On many patterns you will find two bust or chest measurements. The first is 'to fit', meaning the measurement taken from the body. The second is 'actual measurement', meaning the actual size that the finished garment will be, often allowing a few extra centimetres or inches for ease of movement.

Body landmarks

Body circumference:

1 **Bust** – fullest part of the bust (keep level)

2 **Waist** – 2.5cm (1in) above the navel

3 **Hip** – fullest part of the body

Front bodice:

4 **Centre front (CF) neck** – length from front base of neck to waist

5 **CF shoulder** – from base of neck at shoulder point to waist, over bust

6 **Shoulder** – from base of neck to tip of shoulder

7 **Neck** – all around base of neck

8 **Centre shoulder to bust** – centre of the shoulder to apex of the bust

Back bodice:

9 **Centre back (CB) neck** – neck to waist; find the large bone at the CB of your neck down to the CB waist

10 **CB shoulder** – from base of neck at shoulder point to waist

11 **Back** – lower torso (bust line to waist)

Arm:

12 **Upper arm** – all around your upper arm

13 **Arm length** – shoulder to wrist measured with arm slightly bent

14 **Cuff** – all around your wrist

15 **Underarm length** – measurement from the armpit to the wrist

SEE ALSO
Measuring an existing garment
An alternative to taking body measurements is detailed on page 30.

Photocopy this

Mark all your measurements down: remember to re-measure if your body changes shape over time.

MEASUREMENT CHART

Landmark		Standard Size UK12/US8	Personal Measurements
1	Bust	87cm (34¼in)	
2	Waist	68cm (26¾in)	
3	Hip	92cm (36¼in)	
4	CF neck to waist	32cm (12½in)	
5	CF shoulder to waist	34.5cm (13½in)	
6	Shoulder	9cm (3½in)	
7	Neck	37cm (14½in)	
8	Centre shoulder to bust	23cm (9in)	
9	CB neck to waist	40cm (15¾in)	
10	CB shoulder to waist	42cm (16½in)	
11	Back	23.5cm (9¼in)	
12	Upper arm	34cm (13½in)	
13	Arm length	56.5cm (22¼in)	
14	Cuff	17cm (6¾in)	
15	Underarm length	48cm (18⅞in)	

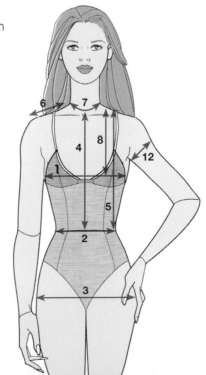

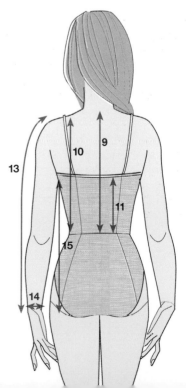

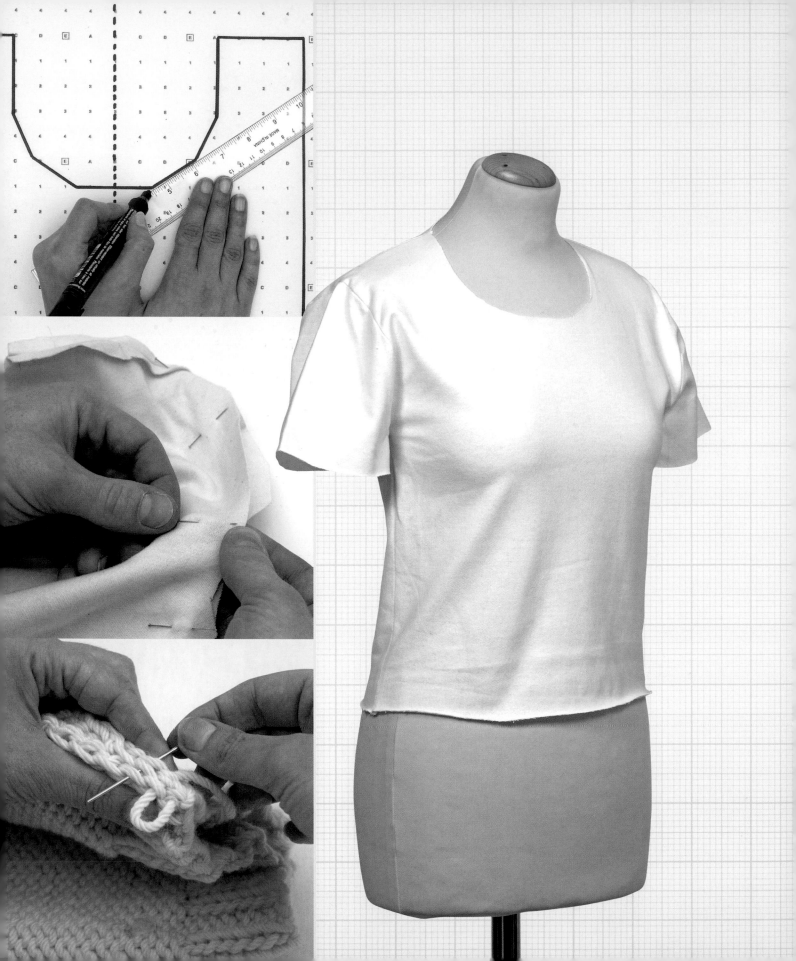

Part 2:
Designing patterns from scratch

In this section you will be shown everything you need to know to design your own patterns from scratch. With the aid of demonstrations and step-by-step exercises, you will learn the skills needed to ensure that your knitted garment fits you perfectly. The inclusion of easy-to-use tables and diagrams means you will be able to calculate and write your own clear and concise knitting patterns.

MAKING A PATTERN FROM AN EXISTING GARMENT

This can be a very useful technique if you have an item that fits you well and that you would like to interpret into a knitted garment.

Measuring an existing garment

This is an alternative method to taking body measurements.

The first thing you need to do is measure your garment correctly. Pick a garment that fits you well. In this instance the measurements are being taken from a jersey T-shirt, size UK12/US8.

You will need

- Existing garment, in this case a T-shirt
- Tape measure
- Paper and pencil
- Tension swatch (see pages 32–33)

Measure your garment

1 Lay your T-shirt flat on a clean, dry surface. Smooth out all wrinkles and ensure that seams are lying flat. Lay a tape measure across the garment, ensuring that it is right up to the edge. Try to be as accurate as possible with your measurements.

2 Refer to the diagram opposite for details of where to measure your garment, and use the chart on page 33 to list the measurements taken.

Keep it simple

Remember that knitting is rarely shaped by darts, so when choosing a garment to measure it's best not to pick a tailored piece. This method will work best with garments that have a simple construction, such as jersey pieces. Tailored knitting is for the more advanced knitter and requires a basic knowledge of pattern cutting.

Taking the measurements

Lay your T-shirt flat: to get an accurate measurement, ensure that your seams are central and that there are no wrinkles in the fabric. Write your results in the chart provided on page 33. Decide whether you are working in centimetres or inches, then stick to that throughout.

A Hem width
This measurement will be converted to give the number of stitches you will need to cast on.

B Hem to armhole
This measurement will give you the information for the number of rows to knit to reach the armhole shaping.

C Armhole to armhole
This measurement will give you the information to calculate the number of stitches you need to decrease to achieve your armhole shaping.

D Armhole to shoulder
This measurement will give you the information to calculate the number of rows needed between the armhole and the shoulder.

E Front neckline depth
This measurement will give you the information on when to start shaping the front neckline.

F Shoulder width
This measurement will give you the information on how many stitches will remain at each side after shaping your neckline.

G Neck width
This measurement will give you the number of stitches across the width of the front neckline. You will also need to consider the shape of the neckline.

H Hem of the sleeve
This measurement will give you the number of stitches to cast on for your sleeve. Remember you are measuring the sleeve on the fold so the flat measurement must be doubled to make H.

I Length of the sleeve
This measurement will give you the total amount of rows to be knitted from the sleeve hem to the sleeve cap.

J Underarm measurement
This measurement will give you the amount of rows to be knitted from the sleeve hem to the armhole point.

K Bicep measurement
This measurement will give you the amount of stitches to be worked for the bicep circumference.

L Bicep to sleeve cap
This measurement will give you the amount of rows to be worked from the bicep point to the top of the sleeve cap.

M Top of sleeve cap
This measurement will give you the amount of stitches to be bound off to finish the sleeve cap. Measure the flat edge of the top of the garment sleeve.

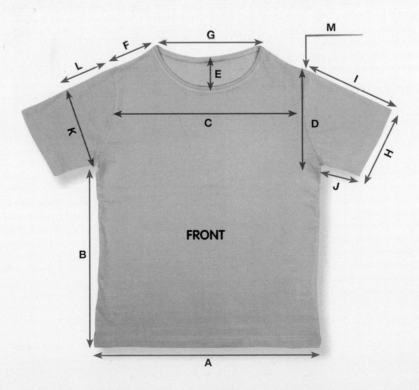

FRONT

Converting the T-shirt measurements into stitches and rows

Our tension swatch gave us this conversion rate:

Stitches
1cm = 1.4 stitches or
1in = 3.5 stitches

Rows
1cm = 1.8 rows or
1in = 4.5 rows

Use these figures to convert your measurements into stitches and rows. For example:

A The hem of the T-shirt (use stitches) converts like this:
40cm x 1.4 sts = 56 sts (40 x 1.4) or
16in x 3.5 sts = 56 sts (16 x 3.5)

So on the pattern made from the size UK12/US8 T-shirt, you would need to cast on 56 stitches. Repeat this calculation to fill out the chart using your own tension conversion. Use the colour coding to decide whether you need to multiply by the row count or the stitch count. It is usually a good idea to round up any odd numbers to even numbers throughout.

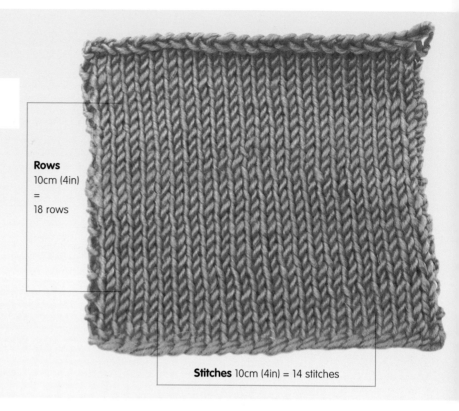

Rows
10cm (4in)
=
18 rows

Stitches 10cm (4in) = 14 stitches

Tip

You may find it helpful to sketch outlines of the pieces and write on the stitches and rows.

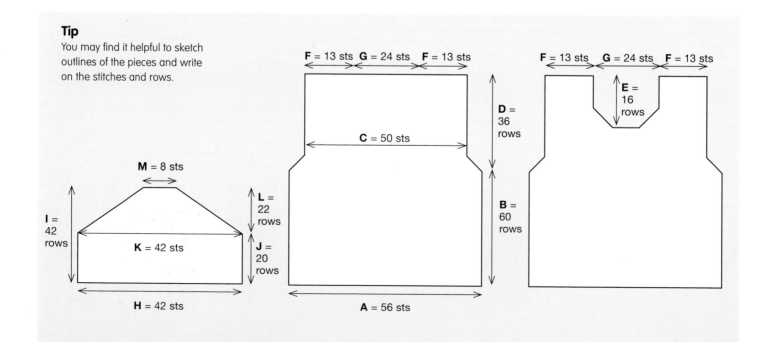

M = 8 sts

I = 42 rows

K = 42 sts

H = 42 sts

F = 13 sts   G = 24 sts   F = 13 sts

C = 50 sts

L = 22 rows

J = 20 rows

A = 56 sts

D = 36 rows

B = 60 rows

F = 13 sts   G = 24 sts   F = 13 sts

E = 16 rows

Photocopy this

Mark all your measurements down here.
You can photocopy it and reuse it for future
patterns so you have a record of your work.

T-shirt measurements to take	Example T-shirt: standard UK12/US8	Your T-shirt measurements	Example in stitches/rows	Your T-shirt in stitches/rows	Sample tension
A Hem width	40cm (16in)		56 sts		10cm (4in) = 14 stitches and 10cm (4in) = 18 rows
B Hem to armhole	33.5cm (13.3in)		60 rows		
C Armhole to armhole	36cm (14.6in)		50 sts		so:
D Armhole to shoulder	20cm (8in)		36 rows		1cm = 1.4 sts / 1.8 rows and
E Front neckline depth	9cm (3.6in)		16 rows		1in = 3.5 sts / 4.5 rows
F Shoulder width	9.2cm (3.8in)		13 sts		
G Neck width	17.5cm (7in)		24 sts		**First step: Your tension**
H Hem of the sleeve	30cm (12in)		42 sts		10cm (4in) = … stitches and 10cm (4in) = … rows
I Length of the sleeve	23.5cm (9in)		42 rows		
J Underarm length	11.5cm (4.4in)		20 rows		so:
K Bicep circumference	30cm (12in)		42 sts		1cm = … sts / … rows and
L Bicep to sleeve cap	12cm (4.6in)		22 rows		1in = … sts / … rows
M Top of sleeve cap	6cm (2.3in)		8 sts		

Key

Horizontal measurements   – Convert to stitches

Vertical measurements   – Convert to rows

Round up your numbers

It is usually convenient to round
up all the numbers of stitches
and rows to EVEN numbers.
This makes shaping
calculations easier.

Converting the measurements

By converting your own measurements, you will have a clearer understanding of how to write your own pattern.

You will need
- Completed table and/or sketches with measurements converted into stitches and rows (see pages 32–33)
- Calculator
- Paper and pencil

In this section you will be shown how to use your measurements to create a basic written pattern and identify areas of shaping. The measurements are taken from the table on page 33.

In this demonstration the pattern will be written out in full. An easy-to-use version with blank spaces for you to fill in your own measurements can be found below.

Rounding up and down

When writing a pattern, you will usually need to round your calculations up or down to even numbers of stitches or rows. For example, 7.7 would be rounded up to 8 and 6.3 rounded down to 6. 7 could be rounded up to 8, or down to 6.

Writing the pattern

Refer to your completed table to find the numbers of stitches and rows for your basic knitting pattern. Note: The words in **bold grey text** are the pattern instructions, as given in the box below.

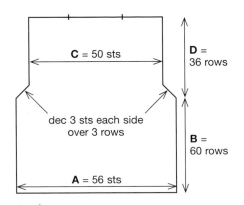

C = 50 sts

D = 36 rows

dec 3 sts each side over 3 rows

B = 60 rows

A = 56 sts

Back

A is the width at the hem, convert this into stitches:
40cm x 1.4 = 56 sts (16in x 3.5 = 56 sts).
Cast on 56 sts.
B is the length to the armhole point, convert this length into rows:
33.5cm x 1.8 = 60 rows
(13.3in x 4.5 = 60 rows).

Work 60 rows.
Shape armholes:
C is the shoulder-to-shoulder width above the armholes, which is converted to stitches:
36cm x 1.4 = 50 sts (14.6in x 3.5 = 50 sts).
Subtract this width from the hem width:
A – C = 56 – 50 = 6 sts. (If your result is not an even number, round it up because these stitches must be divided between the two sides.)
In our example, 3 sts must be decreased at each side.
Decrease 1 st at each end of next 3 rows.
50 sts remain. 63 rows are complete. *
The length of the armhole D converts as follows:
20cm x 1.8 = 36 rows
(8in x 4.5 = 36 rows).
However, 3 of these rows have already been worked during the shaping. So in this case, 36 – 3 = 33 rows remain to the shoulder point. (There is no back neck or shoulder shaping.)
The total length is B + D = 60 + 36 = 96 rows.
Work 33 rows. 96 rows are complete.
Cast off.

Photocopy this

Photocopy this pattern and fill in your own figures in the spaces.

Back

Cast on ... sts.
Work ... rows.
Shape armholes
Decrease 1 st at each end of next ... rows.
... sts remain. ... rows are complete. *
Work ... rows. ... rows are complete.
Cast off.

Front

Work as for back to *.
Work ... rows. ... rows are complete.
Shape front neck: First side
Work ... sts. Turn and work on these sts only.
... rows are complete.
Decrease 1 st at neck edge on next ... rows.
... sts remain. ... rows are complete.
Work ... rows. ... rows are complete.
Cast off remaining ... sts.
Shape front neck: Second side
Rejoin yarn at right of remaining sts, cast off ... sts at centre, work to end of row.
Complete to match first half, reversing shaping.

Cap sleeve

Cast on ... sts.
Work ... rows.
Shape sleeve head
Work ... row. Decrease 1 st at each end of next ... rows. ... sts remain. (... shaping rows).
Repeat these ... rows, ... more times.
... sts remain. (... shaping rows).
Work ... row. Decrease 1 st at each end next ... rows. ... sts remain. ... shaping rows are complete, making ... rows in all.
Cast off remaining ... sts.

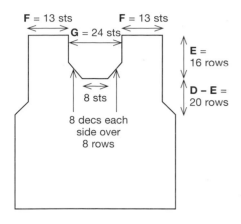

F = 13 sts   F = 13 sts
G = 24 sts
E = 16 rows
D – E = 20 rows
8 sts
8 decs each side over 8 rows

Front

The front is the same shape as the back, up to the end of the armhole shaping. You can put in a star (*) at the end of the instructions for the armhole shaping on the back, and write:

Work as for back to *.

The front neck drop E is converted into rows:

9cm x 1.8 = 16 rows (3.7in x 4.5 = 16 rows).
To find where the front neck shaping begins, subtract this number from the total length:
B + D – E = 96 – 16 = 80 rows.
The armhole shaping ends at 63 rows, so 80 – 63 = 17 rows must be worked to the beginning of the front neck shaping.
Work 17 rows. 80 rows are complete.
Shape front neck: first side.
Check that the stitches for the neck and shoulders add up to the shoulder-to-shoulder width C: G (neck width) + F (shoulder width) + F (shoulder width) = 24 + 13 + 13 = 50 sts (= C).
As a rule of thumb, for a rounded neckline, one-third of G will be cast off at the centre, and one-third decreased at each side of the neck. In this case, G divided by 3 = 8 sts for each group, but you may need to adjust your numbers so that the two decreasing groups are equal.
The neck shaping is worked in two halves, beginning with the left side (as worn). Add the shoulder stitches to the stitches to be decreased on the left side:

F + one-third of G = 13 + 8 = 21 sts.
Work 21 sts. Turn and work on these sts only. 81 rows are complete.
Now work the neck decreases:
Decrease 1 st at neck edge on next 8 rows. 13 sts remain. 89 rows are complete.
Subtract the completed rows from the total length: 96 – 89 = 7 rows.
Work 7 rows. 96 rows are complete.
Cast off remaining 13 sts.
This completes the first (left) half of the neck shaping.
Shape front neck: second side.
Now return to the remaining stitches and cast off one-third of G at the centre:
Rejoin yarn at right of remaining sts, cast off 8 sts at centre, work to end of row.
The second (right) half is then completed to match the first half:
Complete to match first half, reversing shaping.

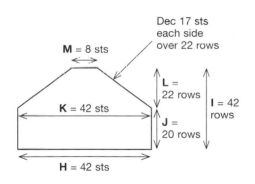

Dec 17 sts each side over 22 rows
M = 8 sts
L = 22 rows
I = 42 rows
K = 42 sts
J = 20 rows
H = 42 sts

Cap sleeve

H is the width of the sleeve hem. Convert this into stitches:
30cm x 1.4 = 42 sts (12in x 3.5 = 42 sts).
Cast on 42 sts.
In this case, the bicep width K is the same as H, so there is no shaping between the hem and the armhole point.
J is the underarm sleeve length, from hem to armhole point, which is converted into rows:
11.5cm x 1.8 = 20 rows (4.6in x 4.5 = 20 rows).
Work 20 rows.
Shape sleeve head.
M is the width at the top of the sleeve head, which is converted to stitches:
6cm x 1.4 = 8 sts (2.3in x 3.5 = 8 sts).
Subtract these stitches from the bicep width:
K – M = 42 – 8 = 34 stitches.
Divide this number by 2 to find the number of stitches to decrease at each side: 17 sts at each side.
L is the depth of the sleeve head, which is total length I minus underarm length J.
L = I – J = 42 – 20 = 22 rows.
Therefore, 17 sts must be decreased at each side, over 22 rows.
If you were to decrease 1 stitch at each end of

every rows 17 times, you would need another 5 rows to reach the length required. Therefore, there will be 5 rows without shaping. These can be evenly spaced as follows: 22 divided by 5 = approx. 4.
This means that there will be one unshaped row for approximately every 4 decreasing rows, which can be written like this:
Work 1 row. Decrease 1 st at each end of next 4 rows. 34 sts remain.
(5 shaping rows).
Repeat these 5 rows, 3 more times.
10 sts remain. (5 + 15 = 20 shaping rows).
Work 1 row. Decrease 1 st at each end next row. 8 sts remain. 22 shaping rows are complete, making 42 rows in all.
Cast off remaining 8 sts.

SEE ALSO
Essential techniques
Casting on, casting off and decreases and increases are detailed on pages 128–135.

Calculating shaping
Shaping a neckline is detailed on pages 38–41.

Making a paper pattern

How to translate your measurements to a full-size paper pattern.

Paper patterns are especially useful because they help you to visualize the garment, and can help you plan your knitting more efficiently to avoid unnecessary mistakes.

Having the pattern drawn out allows you to see where the shaping will take place, and how the garment will look. As you knit the pieces, you can check them against the paper pattern laid flat. You will need a paper pattern if you plan to make a toile (see page 42). The paper pattern can also be used when blocking the garment into shape (see pages 58–61).

For this demonstration the measurements are taken from the example T-shirt on pages 30–33.

You will need
- Garment measurements in centimetres or inches
- Spot-and-cross paper or large sheets of paper
- Pencil
- Ruler
- Set square or pattern master
- Tape measure
- Calculator
- Rough paper for taking notes

Tip
You can use your paper pattern to plot stripes, check that a pattern will repeat in the correct place and try out different necklines. It can be a great tool to test out your designs without the time and effort needed to knit the garment.

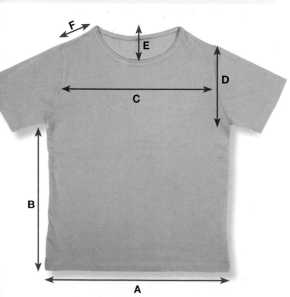

Getting started
Using spot-and-cross paper makes it easy to mark lines both horizontally and vertically, and ensures that the marks are accurately spaced. If you are unable to find spot-and-cross paper, large sheets of newsprint or cheap paper will do.

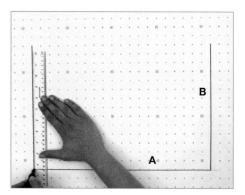

1 A Hem width Lay the paper on a clean, dry surface and ensure that it is flat and that you can reach across the area comfortably. Mark in your first measurement, A, the hem width. Draw a straight line across the bottom of the paper.
B Hem to armhole Use a set square or ruler to line up the right angle on one end of line A, and draw a pencil line up to the correct measurement. Repeat this process on the opposite side.

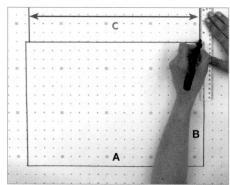

2 C Armhole Draw a straight line across the top of your existing lines to create a box. Subtract measurement C from measurement A and divide the result by 2. From the left, mark this measurement on the top line of your box, and repeat on the right. Draw two lines up from these points. This will give you a squared-off armhole.

Pattern-making paper

There are many types of paper that can be used when making a paper pattern, such as spot-and-cross, alphabet, graph or plain paper. Which type you use is up to personal preference, and each has its own benefits. The marks on the paper can be used to help you line up vertical and horizontal lines on your garment shape. Remember to check that the marks are centred equally. If you use plain paper, it can be helpful to draw a straight line through the centre of the paper, and plot your garment shape so that the line runs vertically through the centre. The line can then be used as a guide for measurements and to help create right angles.

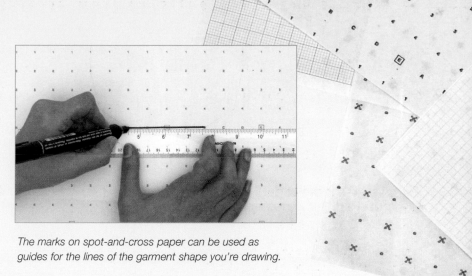

The marks on spot-and-cross paper can be used as guides for the lines of the garment shape you're drawing.

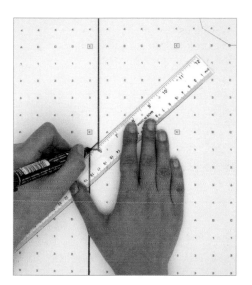

3 If you would like a curved armhole, draw in an equilateral triangle at each armhole.

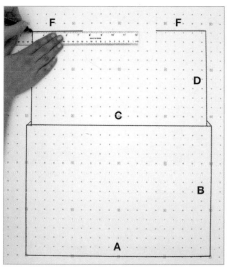

4 D Armhole to shoulder Using a ruler, measure from the armhole to the shoulder. Mark this length (D) on each side. At the shoulder, measure in from the left (and then the right) and mark the shoulder-to-neck measurement (F) on this line.

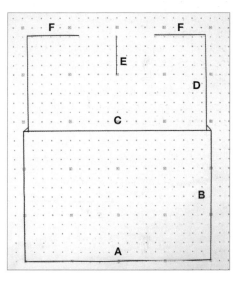

5 E Front neckline depth Mark the centre point between the shoulder lines drawn in step 4. At the marked centre point draw down the measurement for the front neckline depth (E).

SEE ALSO
Blocking and seaming
Methods of using the paper pattern when steaming are detailed on pages 58–61.

Calculating shaping

How to calculate shaping for the neckline and write it into your pattern.

Shaping is a term used to describe either an increase or a decrease in the number of stitches in a row, which determines the overall shape of the piece. The result is a piece of knitting that is shaped to the measurements you require. (See pages 130–133 for a full demonstration of shaping.)

The demonstrations and swatches in this section illustrate how to shape a neckline and how to calculate your pattern.

You will need

- Completed table with measurements converted into stitches and rows (see pages 32–33)
- Calculator
- Spot-and-cross paper, graph paper or plain paper
- Pencil
- Ruler
- Set square

Calculating shaping with triangles

To calculate the shaping of an armhole, neckline or sleeve top, use this triangle method. Where you have drawn a sloping line on the paper pattern, turn it into a triangle as shown.

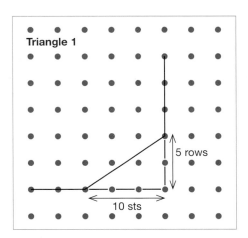

Measure the width of the horizontal line and convert it to stitches. Measure the height of the vertical line and convert it to rows.

Shown here is a triangle 10 stitches wide and 5 rows high. There are more stitches than rows, so more than one stitch will be decreased on each row.

Divide the larger number by the smaller: 10 divided by 5 gives 2. This gives the number of stitches to decrease on each row.

So to shape this sloping edge, decrease 2 sts on each of 5 rows.

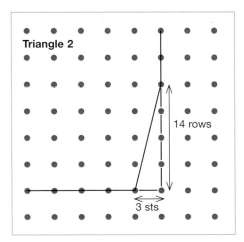

When converted to stitches and rows, this triangle is 3 stitches wide and 14 rows high. There are more rows than stitches, so one stitch will be decreased every few rows.

To find the number of rows per decrease, divide the larger number by the smaller: 14 divided by 3 = 4.6.

If you round this number up to five, you would decrease 1 stitch for every 5 rows: this could be on the 1st, 6th and 11th rows (of 14), or on the 3rd, 8th and 13th.

Shaping a V-neckline

A neckline is usually worked in two halves, one after the other. In this example you will be shown how to shape a V-neck using the calculations taken from the tension swatch on page 33. Right is a simple version of the pattern with blanks left for you to fill in your measurements from a tension swatch of your choice.

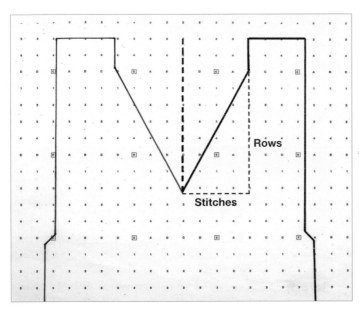

A V-neck is essentially just a large triangle, so the shaping is calculated in the same way as Triangle 2, opposite. Divide whichever is the greater measurement by the smaller, in this case the rows by the stitches, to find the number of rows between the decreases.

Working a V neck

This V-neck neckline is worked in two halves. One half – in this example the left – is calculated and worked, with the stitches that are not being worked secured with a stitch holder or on a spare needle. The process is then repeated on the other side to complete the neckline.

Stitches decreased over rows

Stitches

Rows

V-neck shaping

Photocopy this

Photocopy this V-neck pattern and fill in your own figures in the spaces.

1 After shaping the armholes, work … rows (to required length: total length minus neck depth).

2 Shape first side of the neck: Work … sts (equal to half of total number of sts), turn and work on these sts only, decreasing 1 st on every … row, … times. … sts remain.

3 Work … rows to shoulder point. Cast off.

4 Rejoin yarn at right of remaining sts and complete second side to match first side, reversing the shaping.

A typical V-neck is essentially just a large triangle shape.

Shaping a curved neckline

As with the V-neck example, a curved neckline is also shaped in two halves; you will need to turn the curve into triangles to work out the shaping.

Use the triangle method (see page 38) to work out the shaping for a curved neckline.

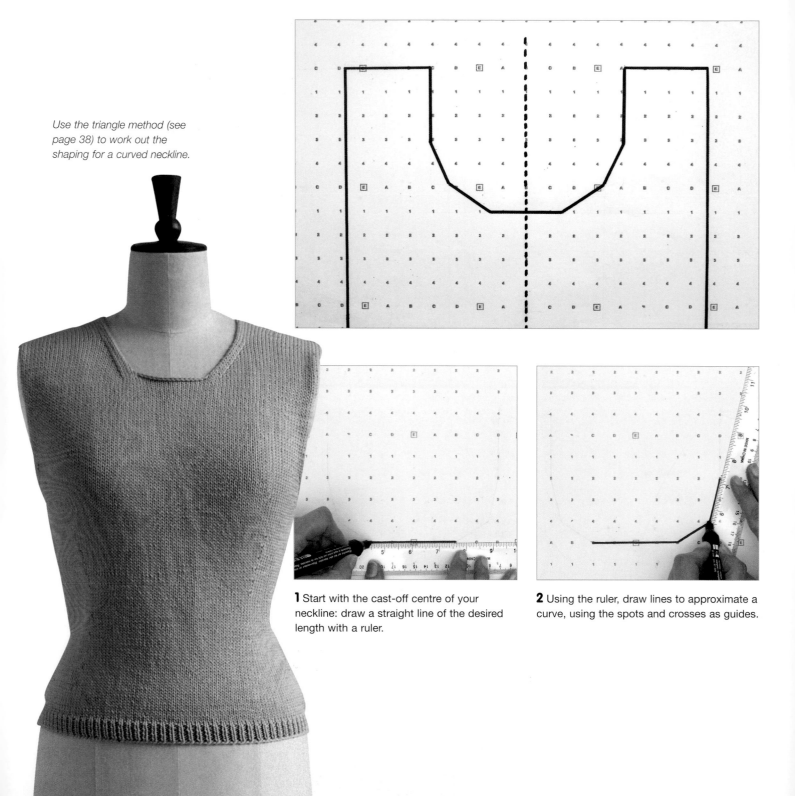

1 Start with the cast-off centre of your neckline: draw a straight line of the desired length with a ruler.

2 Using the ruler, draw lines to approximate a curve, using the spots and crosses as guides.

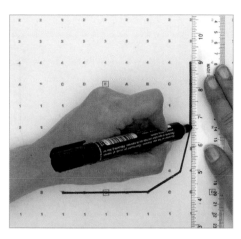

3 Draw a vertical line from your curve to the shoulder point.

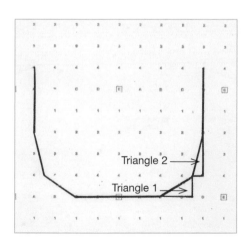

4 When you have completed your neckline, draw in the triangles you will use to calculate your curve for the written pattern.

Triangle 2

Triangle 1

Round-neck shaping

Photocopy this

Photocopy this curved neck pattern and fill in your own figures in the spaces. Use the triangle method (see page 38) to work out the number of decreases needed over the number of rows.

1 After shaping the armhole, work … rows (to required length, which is total length minus neck depth).

2 Shape first side of neck: Work … sts (= shoulder sts plus sts to be decreased at one side), turn and work on these sts only.

3 (Shape triangle 1) Decrease … sts on every … row, … times. … sts remain.

4 (Shape triangle 2) Decrease … sts on every … row, … times. … sts remain (= shoulder sts).

5 Work … rows (to total length required). Cast off.

6 Rejoin yarn at right of remaining sts. Cast off … sts at centre front and complete second side to match first, reversing shaping.

Working a curved neckline

Similar to the V neck on page 39, the curved neckline is worked in two halves. After working the first half, a group of stitches is cast off at the centre, then the second half is completed to match the first half.

No shaping, knit to shoulder

Stitches decreased over rows

Cast-off stitches

Making and fitting a toile

Test the fit of your garment by making a toile and trying it on the body.

'Toile' is a term used in dressmaking to describe a prototype of a garment. Toiles are traditionally produced in calico fabric. They often have no details, such as fastenings or pockets, and instead ideas are drawn directly onto the fabric. When designing for knit, it is best to create the toile in a fabric that has a similar drape and feel to the knitted yarn, such as jersey or synthetic fleece.

You will need

- Paper pattern (see pages 36–37)
- Tape measure
- Pencil
- Ruler or pattern master
- Extra spot-and-cross paper or large sheets of plain paper

Why make a toile?

Toiles are quick to produce and well worth the effort, since a lot of time and work goes into knitting a garment, and it can be heartbreaking to finish a sweater only to find that the fit is unsatisfactory.

If you are working from body measurements without following a garment, it is a good idea to make a toile of the garment first to ensure that you are happy with the fit and feel.

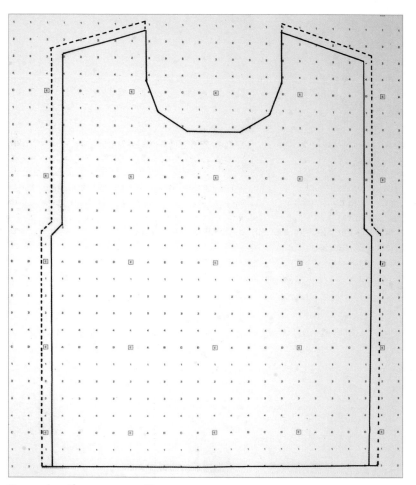

Preparing the paper pattern

In this exercise the paper pattern from pages 36–37 will be used, but with the addition of seam allowances.

Unlike sewing patterns, knitwear patterns do not have seam allowances because the pieces are shaped to the exact size. However, because you are going to sew the toile, you will need to add seam allowances, so mark 1 cm (⅜in) outside the pattern outline where there will be a seam. You can see where this has been done above: the main pattern is drawn in a solid line and the seam allowance in a dashed line. You will sew the toile together with a seam of the same amount.

Drawing the sleeve pattern

You will also need to make a paper pattern for the sleeves. The method below will give a straight sleeve. For a sleeve that is shaped refer to page 76.

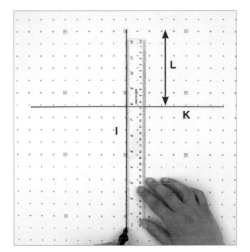

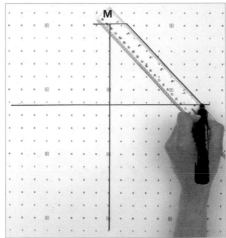

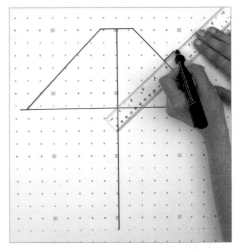

1 Measure from the shoulder point to the cuff or desired length of the sleeves (I) and mark this line on the paper. To create sleeves you will need to calculate the width and height of the sleeve cap. Measure around the bicep to find the circumference (K), and take note of the distance from that point to the shoulder point to ascertain the height of the sleeve cap (L). Mark the bicep measurement horizontally at that point to create a cross.

2 Draw a straight line (M) at the top of the sleeve cap, about 5cm (2in) long. (This measurement can be altered to create different sleeve shapes; see pages 76–87 for design details of sleeves.) Mark about 1.2cm (½in) in from each armhole point, and join these points to each end of M.

3 Measure from armhole to shoulder on your garment. Measure your joining line from step 2 and subtract that measurement from the armhole measurement from your pattern to find the difference in length. Mark a line of this length out from your angled line on the sleeve cap. This line determines the curve of the sleeve cap.

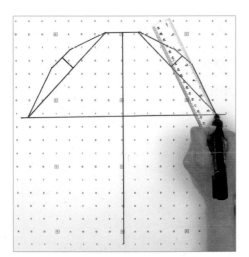

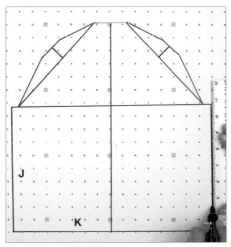

Tip

It is always a good idea to trace patterns and keep a master copy safe. That way if you have to make alterations, or if you make a mistake, you can start again from the master copy.

4 To create the curve of the sleeve cap, you will need to decide how many angles to create. The angles determine the amount of shaping (decrease of stitches over rows). In this example there are 2 angles, making 3 sections to the curve. Repeat on the other side.

5 Draw in the length of the sleeve (J) by marking a vertical line, and draw in the horizontal line at the cuff (K). Add seam allowances where the toile will be seamed.

Sewing your toile together

Now that you have added seam allowances to your paper pattern, you are ready to cut and sew the toile. Try to be as accurate as possible because the resulting toile will be used to represent the finished garment. If you do not wish to make a toile and are happy with your paper pattern, see 'Converting the measurements' on page 34.

You will need

- Jersey or appropriate fabric
- Paper pattern (see pages 36–37)
- Pins
- Weights; you can use tins or cans
- Sewing machine or needle and thread
- Sharp scissors
- Iron and ironing board

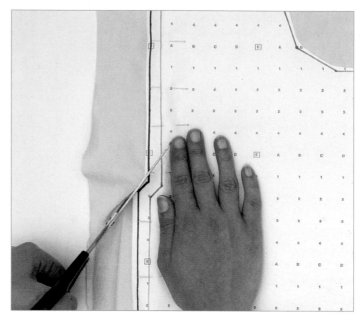

2 Carefully cut out the fabric pieces following the lines on the pattern. Unpin the pattern pieces and remove the fabric.

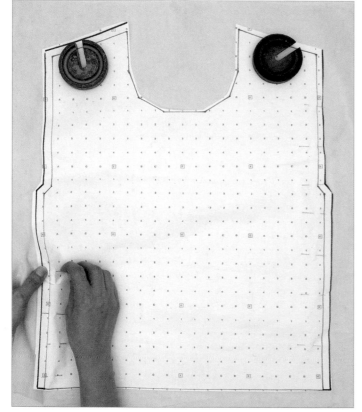

1 Lay your fabric on a flat, dry surface, ensuring you have enough room to work easily. Smooth out all wrinkles. Lay the paper pattern pieces, which should include seam allowances, as detailed on page 42, over the fabric and gently pin it. Be careful not to stretch or distort the fabric when pinning. You may find the fabric easier to control if you place weights at each corner.

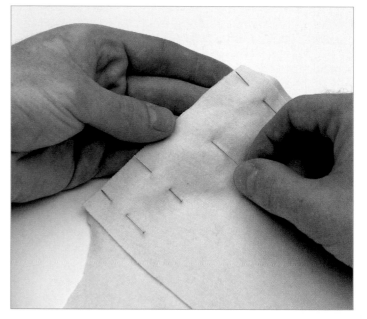

3 Place the front and back pieces with the right sides together. Pin the shoulder points.

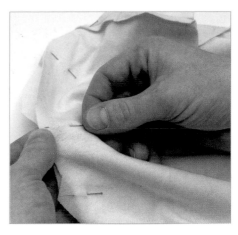

4 Sew all the seams with a seam allowance of 1cm (⅜in), as added to the paper pattern. Sew the two shoulder seams. Open the seams and press flat.

5 With the right sides together, pin the centre of the sleeve cap to the centre point of the shoulder seam. (All seams should end up on the same side.)

6 Pin the edge of the sleeve to the edge of the armhole. Use lots of pins to ensure the sleeve does not slip out of place while being sewn. Sew the sleeve in place. Press the seams open. Sew in the other sleeve in the same way.

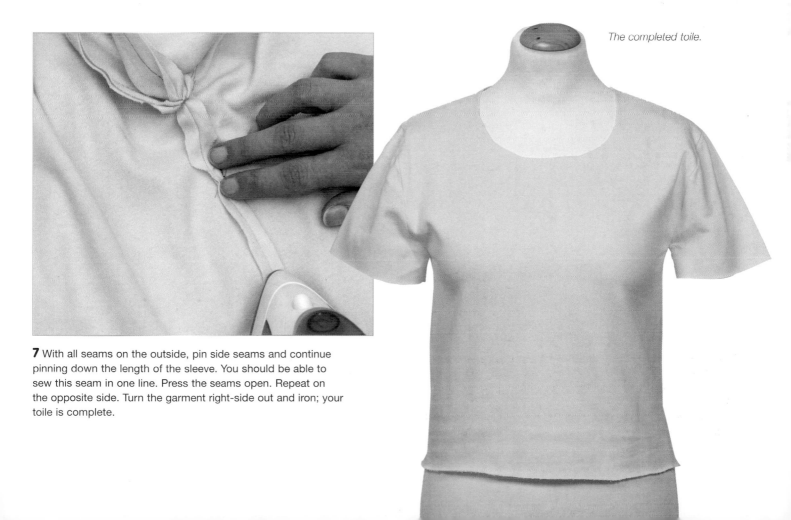

The completed toile.

7 With all seams on the outside, pin side seams and continue pinning down the length of the sleeve. You should be able to sew this seam in one line. Press the seams open. Repeat on the opposite side. Turn the garment right-side out and iron; your toile is complete.

How to
alter a toile

Adapting a toile for perfect fit.

Once you have your toile, you can get a clearer idea of how the garment will look and feel. A toile is a good tool to experiment with. You can alter the fit, sleeve length, body shape and neckline quite easily. In this section we will show you how.

You will need

- Toile (see pages 42–45)
- Paper pattern used for the toile
- Safety pins
- Tape measure
- Paper and pencil for notes
- Pen
- Pins
- Iron and ironing board
- Sewing machine or needle and thread
- Sharp scissors

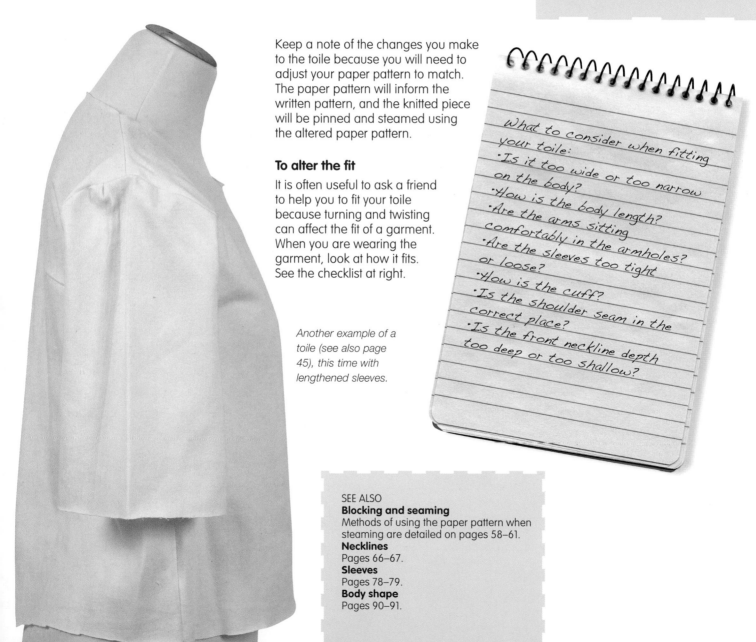

Keep a note of the changes you make to the toile because you will need to adjust your paper pattern to match. The paper pattern will inform the written pattern, and the knitted piece will be pinned and steamed using the altered paper pattern.

To alter the fit

It is often useful to ask a friend to help you to fit your toile because turning and twisting can affect the fit of a garment. When you are wearing the garment, look at how it fits. See the checklist at right.

Another example of a toile (see also page 45), this time with lengthened sleeves.

What to consider when fitting your toile:
- Is it too wide or too narrow on the body?
- How is the body length?
- Are the arms sitting comfortably in the armholes?
- Are the sleeves too tight or loose?
- How is the cuff?
- Is the shoulder seam in the correct place?
- Is the front neckline depth too deep or too shallow?

SEE ALSO
Blocking and seaming
Methods of using the paper pattern when steaming are detailed on pages 58–61.
Necklines
Pages 66–67.
Sleeves
Pages 78–79.
Body shape
Pages 90–91.

Making an alteration

This method can be used for any adjustments. In this example we are adjusting the body width, decreasing it by 1cm (⅜in) each side. After trying the toile on, take the toile off, turn it inside out, measure from the sewn seam inwards and make a mark to the adjusted measurement.

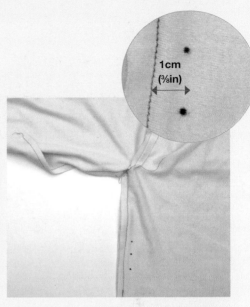

1cm
(⅜in)

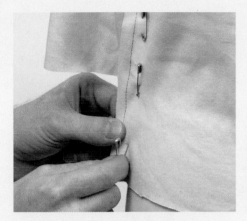

1 With the garment inside out, use safety pins to pin along the new seam line at each side. Turn the garment right-side out and try it on. If it's not quite right, take it off and adjust the safety pins.

2 When you are happy with the adjustment, turn the garment inside out and unpick the seam around the underside of the armhole. Don't forget to make a note of the adjustments you plan to make.

3 Use a pen to mark the toile along the line of safety pins – in this case 1cm (⅜in) in from the seam.

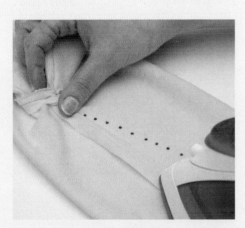

4 Unpick the original sewn seam and iron the fabric flat. Use dressmaking pins to fix the newly positioned seam. Sew the new seam.

5 Pin the sleeve back into place and sew.

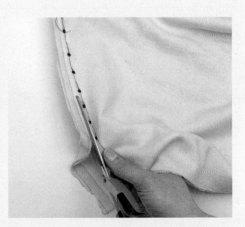

6 Repeat steps 2–5 on the other side. Iron the seams open and cut away any excess fabric. Turn the garment right side out and try on the adjusted toile.

Altering the patterns

After altering the toile, you will need to go back to both your paper pattern and your written pattern and make corresponding alterations.

The paper pattern must be correct because you will be taking measurements from it to write your knitting pattern.

You will need

- Paper pattern used for the toile
- Notes on alterations to be made (see pages 46–47)
- Ruler
- Pen or pencil, preferably in a different colour than that used for the original pattern
- Set square or pattern master
- Tape measure

In this section the method for altering the paper pattern will include decreasing the width of the body, decreasing around an armhole and adjusting the sleeve pattern.

In the previous section, How to alter a toile, you learnt how to decrease the width of the body by 1cm (⅜in) each side. Here you will be shown how to alter the paper pattern to match.

Decreasing the width of the body

Lay the paper pattern flat. Mark 1cm (⅜in) in from the side. Align a ruler or set square at the marked point on the hemline. Draw a line from the hem to the armhole. If you have finished all your alterations, you can either use an eraser to erase the existing line, or mark the new line in a different colour to make the difference easy to follow. Repeat on the other side.

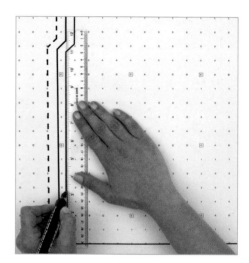

Decreasing around an armhole

When making an adjustment at the armhole, it is important to follow the shaping that already exists. In this demonstration you will be shown how to decrease 1cm (⅜in) around a curved armhole.

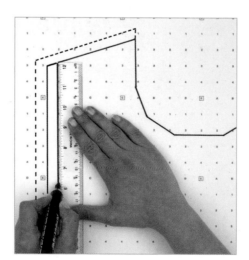

1 Mark in by 1cm (⅜in) at the shoulder. Draw a line down to the armhole point. The armhole pattern has now been decreased by 1cm (⅜in).

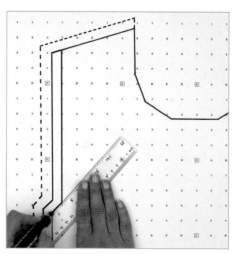

2 Draw in the new armhole shaping line. Repeat on the other side.

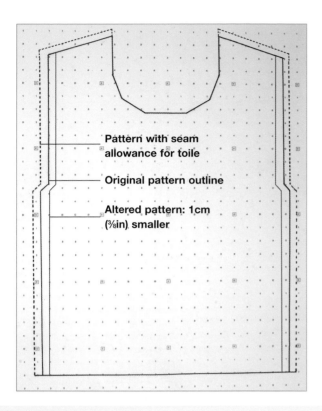

Pattern with seam allowance for toile

Original pattern outline

Altered pattern: 1cm (⅜in) smaller

Your pattern has now been changed to reflect the changes made to the toile.

Tip
Do not cut away parts of the pattern or erase any lines until you have finished all alterations because some existing lines are needed when making adjustments. To avoid confusion, use a different-coloured pen or pencil to mark in the changes.

SEE ALSO
Making a paper pattern
Transferring your measurements to a paper pattern is detailed on pages 36–37.

Sleeve with ease

If you find that the sleeve doesn't quite fit the armhole, you can 'ease' it in. 'Ease' is a term used to describe the distribution of excess fabric when joining a larger piece of fabric to a smaller piece. The excess fabric should be evenly pinned into place to avoid pleating and the pieces joined together with the smaller piece on the top.

When altering a sleeve, there are a number of elements that can be changed, including width measurement at the cuff, sleeve width and sleeve cap, which are all discussed more fully on pages 76–77.

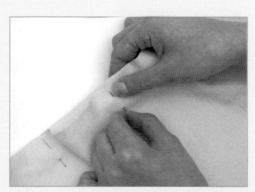

1 Pin the excess fabric evenly.

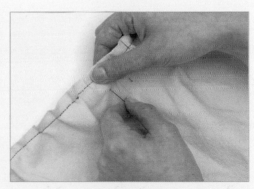

2 Sew the pieces together with the smaller piece on top and then remove the pins.

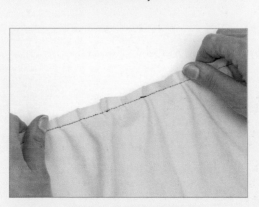

3 The ease should be evenly sewn with no pleats, creating a gently puckered effect.

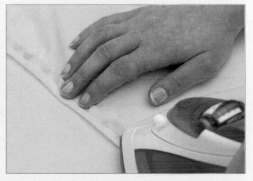

4 Press the seam open.

Writing the pattern: Taking measurements

Once you are happy with your toile and have made the correct alterations to your paper pattern, you can be confident that you have the correct personal measurements to create your knitting pattern.

Ensure that you have a clean, flat area to measure your pattern on. It is important to obtain correct measurements. Lay your pattern flat, and take the following measurements, in the same way as when measuring a garment (see page 30).

You will need

- Adjusted paper pattern (see pages 48–49)
- Tape measure
- Paper and pencil

Measuring the altered pattern

Once you are happy with the fit of your toile, you then transfer the alterations to your paper pattern. Next, you need to take the new measurements from your amended paper pattern.

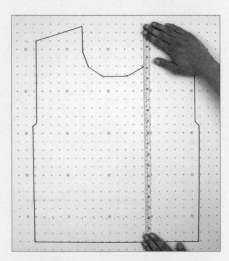

1 Place your altered paper pattern on a clean flat surface and, using a tape measure, take the new measurements.

2 Record your new measurements in a notebook so that you can incorporate them into your written knitting pattern.

Front body pattern

A Hem width
Converts to the number of stitches to cast on.

B Hem to armhole
Converts to the number of rows to be worked to the armhole.

C Armhole to armhole
This will indicate the decrease needed at the armhole.

D Armhole to shoulder
Converts to the number of rows to be worked to the shoulder point.

E Front neckline depth
This will indicate when the shaping for the neckline will start.

F Shoulder width
Converts to the number of stitches to be worked for the shoulder.

G Neck width
C – 2F = G, which converts to the number of stitches for the neckline.

Back body pattern

All the back body measurements are the same as the front, but there is no measurement E.

Sleeve pattern

H Cuff width
Converts to the number of stitches to be cast on for the cuff.

I Sleeve length
Converts to the total number of rows to be worked.

J Underarm length
Converts to the number of rows to be worked to the sleeve cap.

K Width at underarm bicep
Converts to the number of stitches required at this point. (The difference between H and K indicates the increase needed at the side edges.)

L Bicep to sleeve cap
Converts to the rows for the sleeve cap.

M Top of sleeve cap
This will indicate the number of stitches to be bound off at the top of the sleeve.

N Measurement of sleeve cap
This measurement, plus half of M should match the armhole measurement on front and back, measured around the curve.

Now convert your new set of measurements to stitches and rows (as page 33) and then into a new written pattern (see page 34).

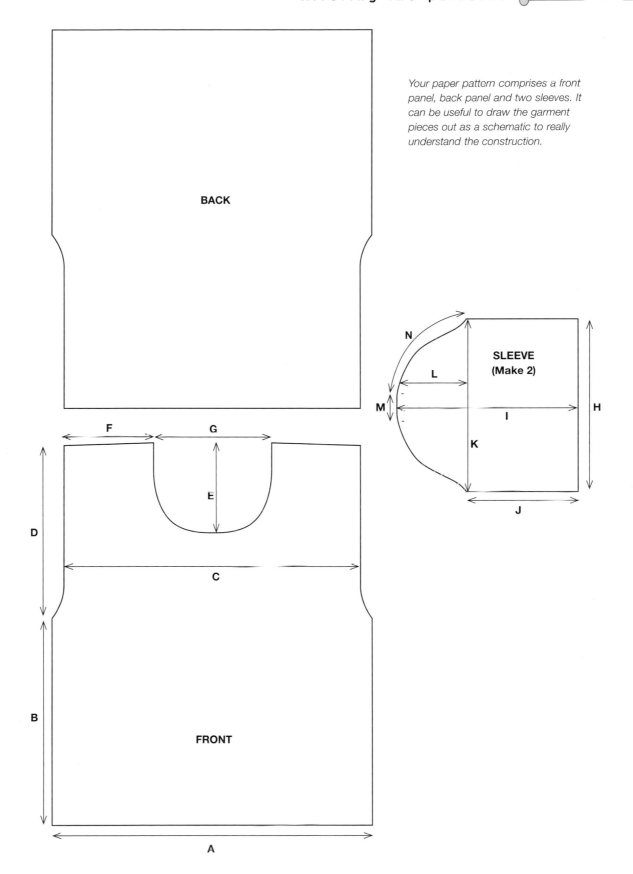

Your paper pattern comprises a front panel, back panel and two sleeves. It can be useful to draw the garment pieces out as a schematic to really understand the construction.

BACK

SLEEVE
(Make 2)

N

L

M

H

I

K

J

F

G

E

D

C

B

FRONT

A

Rewriting the instructions

You will now be able to use your new measurements to calculate the stitches and rows needed to knit your garment.

Now that you have refined the sweater shape by making and fitting a toile, and making corresponding changes to the paper pattern, you can adapt and rewrite the instructions from pages 34–35 to take in your changes.

You will need

- Measurements taken from the paper pattern (see pages 48–50)
- Tension swatch knitted in the yarn to be used for the garment (see pages 20–21)
- Tape measure
- Calculator
- Paper and pencil

For this version of the cap-sleeve sweater, we have made the following changes to the instructions on pages 34–35:
- Adding rib welts to the body and sleeves
- Reducing the shoulder-to-shoulder width by 1cm (⅜in) at each side, so adding more shaping at the armholes
- Shaping the neckline with a graduated curve
- Shaping the underarm sleeve
- Shaping the sleeve cap with a graduated curve

Exact wording

Every designer has their own favourite style for writing pattern instructions; magazines and yarn spinners have a 'house style'. Many instructions may be expressed in more than one way, for example 'Repeat these 2 rows, 3 more times, 20 sts remain' means exactly the same as 'Repeat the last 2 rows until 20 sts remain', but the first wording is rather more precise.

When writing a pattern, be as clear as possible so that the instructions cannot be misread, even if you will be knitting the garment yourself. (You may think you'll remember what you meant, but you won't!) This is even more important if someone else will be knitting the garment – they must be able to understand exactly what you mean.

Converting the measurements

This is the same process as described on page 34.

For this example the tension used is:
1cm = 1.4 sts / 1.8 rows
1in = 3.5 sts / 4.5 rows

Rewrite the pattern

Note: The words in **bold grey text** are the pattern instructions as given in the box on page 56.

Tip
If you write on a computer, it's easy to make changes to the text for your original instructions. But it's also a good idea to save both versions of the pattern – as with the paper pattern, keep the master copy safe, in case you need to return to it in the future.

Back

A is the width at the hem, which converts to 56 sts.

For a rib welt, it is usual to knit the rib on needles about two sizes smaller than the main parts, so the needle size must be specified:

Using size ... needles, cast on 56 sts.

Calculate the number of rib rows required – in this case, 6 rows.

Work in K1, P1 rib for 6 rows.

Don't forget to change to larger needles, and the main stitch, as used for the tension swatch:

Change to size ... needles. Continue in stocking stitch throughout.

B is the length to the armhole point, which converts to 60 rows. Having already knitted 6 rib rows, 54 rows remain to be worked in the main stitch:

Work 54 rows.

Shape armholes

C is the shoulder to shoulder width above the armholes, which converts to 44 stitches. Subtract this width from the hem width:

A – C = 56 – 44 = 12 sts.

Therefore in our example, 6 sts must be decreased at each side. The shape of a set-in armhole often begins with a short horizontal section, which is shaped by casting off a small group of stitches at the beginning of the next 2 rows (that is, one group at the beginning of the right-side row, and one group at the beginning of the following wrong-side row). In our example, each group is 2 sts wide:

Cast off 2 sts at beginning next 2 rows. 52 sts remain (2 shaping rows complete).

The slope of the remaining decreasing should be calculated using the triangle method (page 39). In this case, 4 sts must be decreased (at each side) over 6 rows, giving the instructions:

Decrease 1 st at each end next 2 rows.

Work 1 row. Decrease 1 st at each end next row.

Repeat the last 2 rows once more. 44 sts remain. * (2 + 6 = 8 shaping rows complete).

The length of the armhole D converts to 36 rows. 8 of these rows have already been worked during the shaping. So in this case, 36 – 8 = 28 rows remain to the shoulder point. (There is no back neck or shoulder shaping.)

The total length is B + D = 60 + 36 = 96 rows.

Work 28 rows. 96 rows are complete. Cast off.

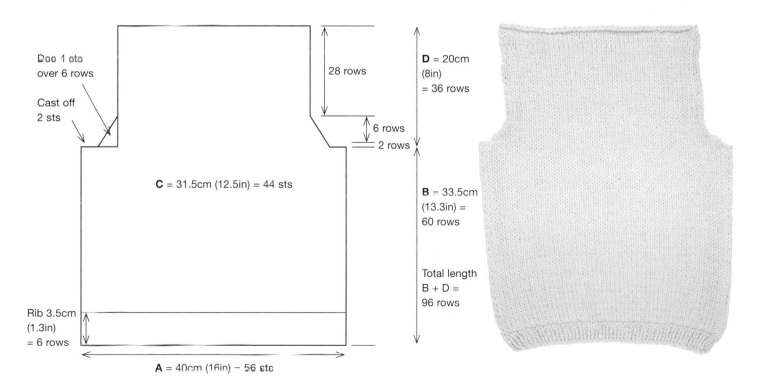

Dec 1 sts over 6 rows

Cast off 2 sts

28 rows

6 rows
2 rows

D = 20cm (8in) = 36 rows

C = 31.5cm (12.5in) = 44 sts

B = 33.5cm (13.3in) = 60 rows

Total length B + D = 96 rows

Rib 3.5cm (1.3in) = 6 rows

A = 40cm (16in) = 56 sts

Front

The front is the same shape as the back, up to the end of the armhole shaping. You can put in a star (*) at the end of the instructions for the armhole shaping on the back, and write:

Work as for back to *.

The front neck drop E converts to 16 rows. To find where the front neck shaping begins, subtract this number from the total length:

B + D – E = 96 – 16 = 80 rows.

The armhole shaping ends at 68 rows, so 80 – 68 = 12 rows must be worked to the beginning of the front neck shaping.

Work 12 rows. 80 rows are complete.

Shape front neck: first side

Check that the stitches for the neck and shoulders add up to the shoulder-to-shoulder width C: G (neck width) + F (shoulder width) + F (shoulder width) = 22 + 11 + 11 = 44 sts (= C).

8 sts will be bound off at the centre front, leaving 7 sts to be decreased at each side. Add these sts to the shoulder sts: F + sts to be decreased = 11 + 7 = 18 sts.

Work 18 sts. Turn and work on these sts only. (1 neck row complete.)

Now work the neck decreases: For a nicely rounded curve, shape the decreasing using 2 triangles of different proportions, as shown. Calculate the shaping of each triangle as on pages 40–41: on our diagram, the first triangle represents 4 sts decreased over 4 rows, and the second triangle, 3 sts decreased over 6 rows.

Decrease 1 st at neck edge on next 4 rows. 14 sts remain. (5 neck rows complete.)

Work 1 row. Decrease 1 st at neck edge on next row.

Repeat the last 2 rows twice more. 11 sts remain. (11 neck rows complete.) 91 rows complete in all.

Subtract the completed rows from the total length:

96 – 91 = 5 rows.

Work 5 rows. 96 rows are complete.

Cast off remaining 11 sts.

This completes the first (left) half of the neck shaping.

Shape front neck: second side

Now return to the remaining stitches and cast off the centre group of sts:

Rejoin yarn at right of remaining sts, cast off 8 sts, work to end of row.

The second (right) half is then completed to match the first half:

Complete to match first half, reversing shaping.

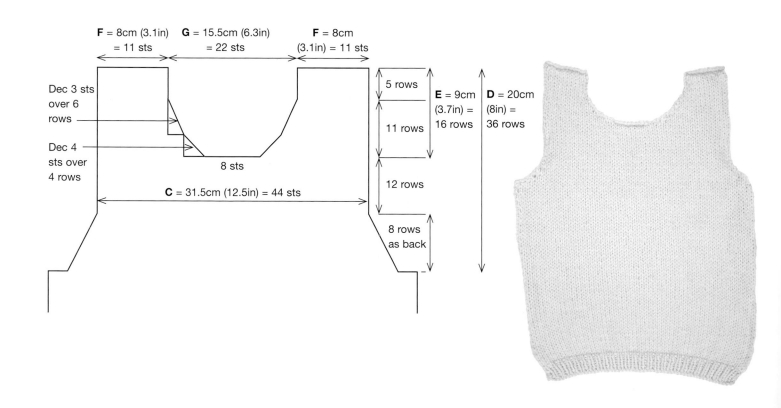

Cap sleeve

H is the width of the sleeve hem, which gives 34 stitches. We are going to knit the first 4 rows in rib:
Using size … needles, cast on 34 sts. Work 4 rows K1, P1 rib.
Change to size … needles and work in stocking stitch throughout.
K is the bicep width, which converts to 42 stitches, therefore:
K – H = 42 – 34 = 8 sts must be increased to reach the bicep width.
Divide this number by 2: 4 sts will be increased at each side.
J is the underarm sleeve length, from hem to armhole point, which converts to 20 rows; however, 4 of these rows have already been worked, so 16 rows remain to the bicep point.
4 sts will be increased at each edge over 16 rows. Spread the increases evenly: 16 divided by 4 = 4.

Increase 1 st at each end next and following 4th row, 4 times in all. 42 sts. (4 + 13 = 17 rows complete.)
Work 3 rows. 20 rows complete.
Shape sleeve head
M is the width at the top of the sleeve head, which converts to 8 stitches. Subtract these stitches from the bicep width:
K – M = 42 – 8 = 34 stitches.
Divide this number by 2 to find the number of stitches to decrease at each side: 17 sts at each side. Begin by casting off a small group of sts at each side, to match the beginning of the armhole shaping on front and back:
Cast off 2 sts at beginning next 2 rows. 38 sts remain. 2 shaping rows complete.

L is the depth of the sleeve head, which is 22 rows. Subtract the 2 shaping rows already worked:
22 – 2 = 20 shaping rows remain.
15 more sts must be decreased at each side, over 20 rows.
Use the triangle method to calculate the shaping for the curve you want on the sleeve head. In our example, the first triangle represents 5 sts decreased over 10 rows (at each side):
Decrease 1 st at each end of next row. Work 1 row.
Repeat these 2 rows, 4 more times. 28 sts remain. (2 + 10 = 12 shaping rows complete.)
The second triangle represents 10 sts decreased over 10 rows (at each side):
Decrease 1 st at each end of next 10 rows. 8 sts remain. (12 + 10 = 22 shaping rows complete).
Cast off.

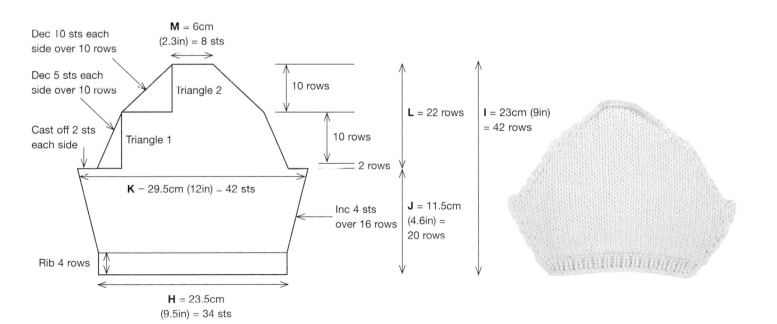

Dec 10 sts each side over 10 rows

Dec 5 sts each side over 10 rows

Cast off 2 sts each side

M = 6cm (2.3in) = 8 sts

Triangle 2

Triangle 1

10 rows

10 rows

2 rows

L = 22 rows

I = 23cm (9in) = 42 rows

K – 29.5cm (12in) – 42 sts

Inc 4 sts over 16 rows

J = 11.5cm (4.6in) = 20 rows

Rib 4 rows

H = 23.5cm (9.5in) = 34 sts

Photocopy this

Photocopy this pattern and fill in your own figures in the spaces.

Tension: Using size … needles,
1cm = … sts / … rows
1in = … sts / … rows
Rib worked on size … needles.

Back

Using size … needles, cast on … sts.
Work in K1, P1 rib for … rows.
Change to size … needles. Continue in stocking stitch throughout.
Work … rows.
Shape armholes
Cast off … sts at beginning next 2 rows. … sts remain.
(2 shaping rows complete.)
Decrease 1 st at each end next … rows.
Work 1 row. Decrease 1 st at each end next row.
Repeat the last 2 rows … more times. … sts remain.
(2 + … = … shaping rows complete.) *
Work … rows. … rows are complete.
Cast off.

Front

Work as for back to *.
Work … rows. … rows are complete.
Shape front neck: First side
Work … sts. Turn and work on these sts only. (1 neck row complete.)
Decrease 1 st at neck edge on next … rows. … sts remain.
(… neck rows complete.)
Work 1 row. Decrease 1 st at neck edge on next row.
Repeat the last 2 rows … more times. … sts remain.
(… neck rows complete.) … rows complete in all.
Work … rows. … rows are complete.
Cast off remaining … sts.
Shape front neck: Second side
Rejoin yarn at right of remaining sts, cast off … sts, work to end of row.
Complete to match first half, reversing shaping.

Cap sleeve

Using size … needles, cast on … sts.
Work … rows K1, P1 rib.
Change to size … needles and work in stocking stitch throughout.
Increase 1 st at each end next and following … row, … times in all.
… sts. (… + … = … rows complete.)
Work … rows. … rows are complete.
Shape sleeve head
Cast off … sts at beginning next 2 rows. … sts remain. 2 shaping rows complete.
Decrease 1 st at each end of next row. Work 1 row.
Repeat these 2 rows, … more times. … sts remain.
(2 + … = … shaping rows complete.)
Decrease 1 st at each end of next … rows. … sts remain.
(… + … = … shaping rows complete.)
Cast off.

Note

Now you can add the neck finish of your choice: a crew or rolled neck, frill or collar – see page 64 for more ideas.

Charting shaping

When working out shapings for necklines and sleeves, there are often several possible ways of fitting the shaping to the required rows. If you find this confusing, try charting the increases and decreases on graph paper, using one square of graph paper to represent one stitch. This diagram shows the cap sleeve from the written pattern.

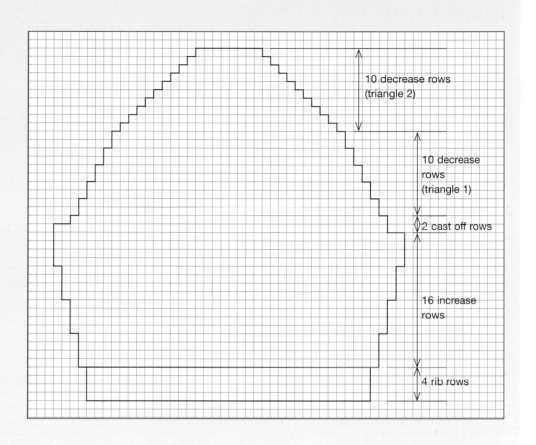

10 decrease rows (triangle 2)

10 decrease rows (triangle 1)

2 cast off rows

16 increase rows

4 rib rows

Once you have the individual pieces you can move on to constructing your garment, see page 58.

CONSTRUCTING THE GARMENT

When you have knitted the elements of your pattern – front, back and sleeves – these pieces need to be treated and sewn together. How you press and construct your knitted pieces will affect the overall look of the garment.

Blocking and seaming

Attention to the small details when blocking your pieces and stitching the seams will add to the design and leave you with a professionally finished item.

There are two main ways to block your pieces. Steaming is known as the dry method, while the wet method involves either spraying the pieces with water or immersing them. Steaming gives garments a professional finish, helps to settle the stitches, and can even out irregularities. However, oversteaming your knitting can make it lifeless and limp.

You will need

- Knitted pieces
- Pins
- Paper pattern used to create the knitted pieces
- Tape measure
- Ironing board, plus towel and cotton sheet for larger pieces

Wet spray or blocking method
- Spray bottle or bowl of water and mild detergent
- Extra yarn
- Yarn or tapestry needle

Pressing method
- Iron
- Cotton cloth

Preparing the blocking surface

If the pieces are small, you may be able to press them on an ironing board. Otherwise, you can prepare a blocking area by laying a towel flat on a table and covering it with a clean, dry cotton sheet, ensuring that there are no wrinkles.

Pinning the knitting

Lay your knitting right side down on the prepared surface. Refer to the measurements from your pattern and use a tape measure to check that you have pinned each piece to the correct size. Be careful not to pull the knitting too tightly. The shape you block is the shape that will stay.

You may find it easier to pin the pieces to the paper pattern. Ensure that the paper is clean because ink marks can be easily transferred with steam.

Ribbed areas should not be pinned; if they are stretched and pinned they will lose their elasticity and not return to their previous appearance.

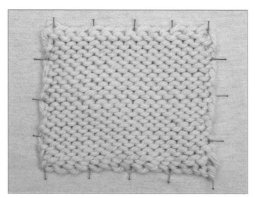

In this example, the knitting has been incorrectly pinned – the stitches are pulled and distorted.

Here, the swatch is correctly pinned. It is taut enough for the shape to be correct but not distorted.

Wet spray method (right)

Pin the pieces into shape. With a spray bottle, mist water evenly over your knitting until it is damp. Pat the water into the knitted fabric to ensure that it penetrates the yarn. Leave the knitting to dry naturally, and unpin when completely dry.

Blocking method

For the blocking method, gently wash the knitted pieces in a bowl with warm water. It is safest to use a special detergent. Squeeze the knitting rather than rubbing, which can cause wool fibres to felt.

Rinse the pieces in cool water and ensure that all the detergent is removed. Avoid lifting the pieces since they will be heavy with water and may stretch. Do not wring out; instead push the water out.

Lay the knitting flat on a towel and roll up to squeeze out the excess water, then pin to the board and leave to dry as above.

Pressing method (left)

Set the iron to the temperature advised on the ball band and check the band to see whether you are required to use a dry iron or an iron with steam. It is best to not use an iron directly on the knitting, but to lay a piece of clean cotton cloth over the knit. Some ball bands will advise using a damp cloth. In this case, run a clean cotton cloth under cold water and wring it out so that it is damp, not wet.

Rest the iron gently on the cloth; do not press down or move the iron around. Lift and replace the iron next to the spot where it was resting previously. Repeat this process until the whole piece has been pressed.

To steam rib, lay the knitted piece down and gently steam with the iron held approximately 3cm (1in) above the fabric. The steam will gently set the stitches, but not affect the qualities of the rib.

Remove the cloth and allow the knitting to cool completely before removing the pins.

Movable blocking board

You can prepare a blocking board by pinning or stapling a towel covered by a cotton sheet to a board. This is then movable and can easily be supported and manoeuvred on the ironing board. You can use a checked fabric for a ready-made grid to work on. Never rest your iron on the unfixed board.

Check the yarn ball band

Instructions for how to wash and/or steam your chosen yarn should be shown on the ball band. Some fancy and manmade yarns do not respond well to an iron because synthetic fibres can melt and burn. Always check the yarn ball band before starting these processes.

Assembling your garment

It is best to assemble your garment by hand. Machine sewing is never recommended for hand knitting because the knitted fabric will always stretch or pucker.

There are many different methods of joining knit, some of the most common of which are discussed in the Essential techniques section (see pages 128–135). Some basic rules should be followed when assembling your garment:

- Sew the garment together in the same yarn it has been knitted with to ensure that the stitches will be camouflaged.

- Use a yarn or tapestry needle with an eye large enough to accommodate the yarn and a blunt tip to avoid splitting the yarn.

- Most knitting patterns give an assembly order that should be followed:
  Join shoulder seams
  Join sleeves to armholes
  Join sleeves from the cuff up to armhole
  Join side seams from hem to armholes.

- If the garment is patterned or striped, wherever possible try to join the pieces so that the patterns or stripes match.

- Keep checking as you go along by laying your pieces next to each other and ensuring they fit. If you sew too tightly, you may distort the pieces.

- When sewing from the wrong side, keep checking on the right side of your knitting to ensure that the seam is even and neat.

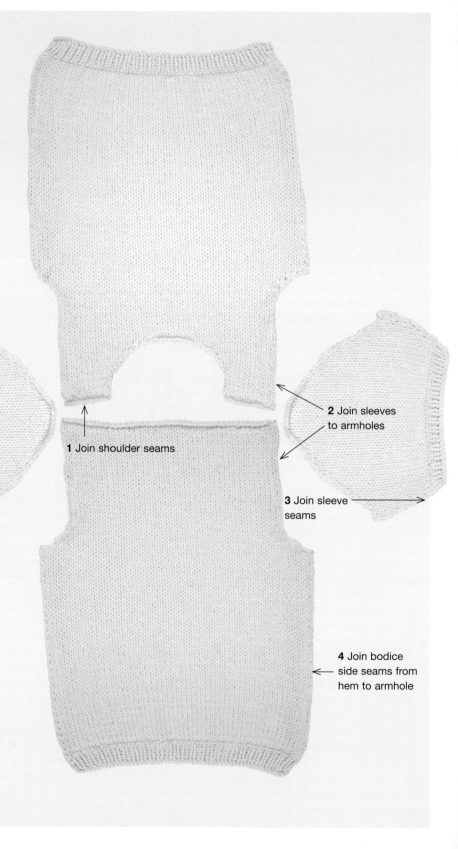

1 Join shoulder seams

2 Join sleeves to armholes

3 Join sleeve seams

4 Join bodice side seams from hem to armhole

Stitching the seams

For a professional finish, spend time assembling your work with care. The stitching method shown below is worked from the wrong side. Other methods are shown on page 135.

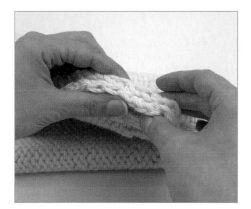

1 With right sides together, press the two edges together to line up the stitches.

2 Thread a needle using the same yarn the garment is made from and pass it towards you from one side to the other, through a stitch from each of the pieces you are joining.

3 Gently pull the yarn through to create a stitch. Do not pull too tightly because this will distort the seam.

4 Pass the needle away from you through the next two stitches; pull through gently.

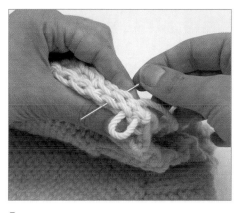

5 Repeat to complete the seam.

The basic assembled garment made to your own measurements. Now, take the next step by adapting the pattern to add design details (pages 62–105) and embellishments (pages 106–119).

Part 3:
How to adapt the pattern

In this chapter you will be shown how to adapt the pattern. Step-by-step demonstrations, illustrated with photography and artworks, demonstrate how to adapt a toile, alter a paper pattern and adapt the written knitting pattern. Examples will show how to change a neckline, alter a sleeve and change the body shape.

CHANGING NECKLINES

Changing a neckline can change the character and function of your knitwear design: from daywear to eveningwear, from practical crew neck pullover to fancy frill-neck sweater.

This neckline is formed from panels of ribbed knitting folded to create volume and structure. The panels are then assembled to form the garment, resulting in an unusual and dramatic piece.

Design options: Necklines

The shape of a neckline can affect the overall styling of a garment.

In many ways, the neckline is the main feature of a garment. By dropping a V-neck by 5cm (2in) and changing the yarn, you can turn a classic daywear sweater into a feminine evening top. Here are some of the more unusual necklines that you may want to use when adapting your own knitting pattern.

Choosing the right shape

The most common neckline used in a knitted garment is the crew neck: a neat fitted round-neck shape with a rib finish. Often, with designer sweaters, small details are added, such as an interesting trim, a tipping of colour or a side opening. You may want to mix the tension of your neckline by using a different weight yarn for your trim – this is a quick way to add an element of interest to your pattern. Alternatively, you could add a highlight colour to make a bold statement.

Designing a neckline

When designing your own sweater, it is important to consider the impact the neckline will have on the overall look. Necklines to consider include: funnel, square, bateau, scoop, envelope, slashed, deep U, roll and many more. When choosing your neckline shape, you should also consider the rest of the garment. For example a raglan sleeve will not work with a wide square neck. The best way to do this is to sketch your garment so that you can consider all the design elements together.

Also, you should consider your choice of yarn at the earliest stage. Knitting a classic sweater shape in an unexpected yarn adds interest and an element of design without making any changes to the pattern.

Keyhole

This attractive neckline works well with knitwear. The slash can be extended by starting the shaping of the neckline at an earlier row.

The keyhole can be joined by a number of methods, the most popular being a simple button. You could also knit two ties, which can be sewn onto the neckline and used to join the neckline with a bow.

Boat neck (bateau)

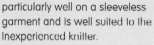

The straight line that cuts across the shoulders is the easiest neckline to knit because it requires no shaping. This style works particularly well on a sleeveless garment and is well suited to the inexperienced knitter.

Envelope

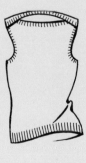

This type of neckline is well suited to the novice knitter; the style requires only a small amount of shaping. A contrast colour on the trim will highlight the detail of the fabric crossing over on the shoulder.

Polo neck

This classic knitted neckline is usually created using a rib stitch, which will pull in to sit snugly around the neck, but also has the ability to stretch over the head. Interest can be added by tipping the rib in a different colour, or by increasing the amount of rows knitted to allow for a more dramatic roll.

Frill

The frill can be knitted separately and sewn onto the garment or knitted integrally. Either method works well but will give different effects. It is a good idea to do a test swatch first to see which technique you prefer.

Drape

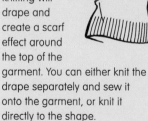

This neckline will work well when using a finer yarn. The excess knitting will drape and create a scarf effect around the top of the garment. You can either knit the drape separately and sew it onto the garment, or knit it directly to the shape.

Shawl collar

This soft collar is often used on cardigans; it can look especially dramatic when oversized. The collar can either be knitted integrally with the garment or sewn on at a later stage. The seaming method can be used if you would like to add interest to your garment by using a different stitch on the collar.

Crew neck

The most classic and commonly seen neckline in knitwear, the crew neck is often ribbed to create a very neat finish; however, it can also be knitted in a different direction and sewn on to add interest.

V-neck

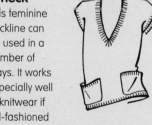

This feminine neckline can be used in a number of ways. It works especially well in knitwear if full-fashioned decreasing is used to highlight the shaping. The neckline can be dropped easily by starting the shaping at an earlier row.

Funnel

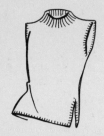

The funnel neckline is created by extending the normal neckline, resulting in a style that can rest at the base of the neck or rise to fit neatly under the chin. This can be achieved by increasing the amount of rows knitted at the neck; funnel necklines can be knitted in two pieces with seams that run from the shoulder, or as one on a circular needle.

Square neck

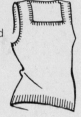

This is a good neckline for the novice knitter. This neckline requires no shaping but does give you the experience of knitting the neck in two stages: one side is knitted first, then the stitches are cast off at the centre, and the second side is knitted last.

Tip

Where a neckline is required to stretch to fit over the head, knit it integrally or attach it with a grafted seam. For a more structured neck edge (for example, to support a large frill or collar), cast off the neck edges, knit the neckline separately and attach with a firm seam.

Necklines:
Adapting the toile

First use your toile to help you choose
your preferred neckline.

A toile helps you to visualize the look of a knitted garment without
actually knitting it. In this section you will be shown how to sample
different necklines on the toile to help you make your design choices.

You can alter your existing toile, or quickly make up several tabards
with different necklines to find the style you want. Ensure that you have
enough room to work on a clear, flat surface. You can mark your
neckline with a pen, pins, masking tape or tacking stitches.

You will need

- Toile (see pages 42–45)
- Tape measure
- Paper and pencil
- Pen, pins, masking tape, or needle
  and thread
- Paper pattern (see pages 36–37) or
  garment (see pages 30–33)
- Jersey or other appropriate fabric
- Iron and ironing board
- Sharp scissors

Using an existing garment

If you have an existing garment
with your preferred neckline you
can take measurements from that
and mark them onto your toile. This
method can be useful if you have
already used a toile to create a
knitted garment and are happy
with the fit but want to create
another garment with
a different neckline.

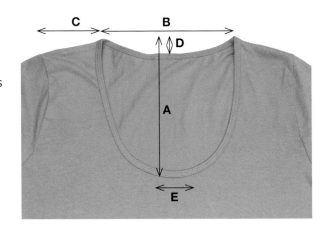

1 Lay the existing garment flat and
make a note of all the measurements
you will need from the neckline. You
will need these measurements to alter
your paper pattern in the next section.
A Front neck drop
B Width of neck
C Shoulder width
D Back neck drop
E Width of centre front neckline

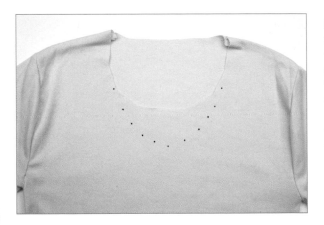

2 Lay your existing toile out flat and
mark all of the measurements from
the garment onto it, using whichever
method you are happiest with. Try on
the toile. If you are happy with the
neckline, cut away the excess fabric.
If not, mark another neckline until you
are satisfied with the effect. Now
adapt the paper pattern; see page 68.

SEE ALSO
Making a paper pattern
Making a paper pattern by
transferring your measurements
is detailed on pages 36–37.

Making and fitting a toile
Detailed instructions on how to
make and assess the fit of a
toile can be found on
pages 42–45.

How to alter a toile
Learn how to adjust a toile
on pages 46–47.

Making a mock neckline

This method can be useful if you do not want to alter your toile but want to experiment with different necklines. The technique involves creating simple jersey tabards with alternative necklines, to ensure that you are happy with a neck's shape and depth.

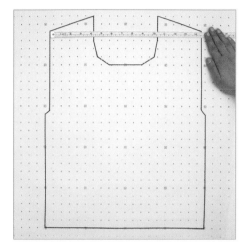

1 Using an existing paper pattern, garment or toile, make a note of the measurement from shoulder to shoulder.

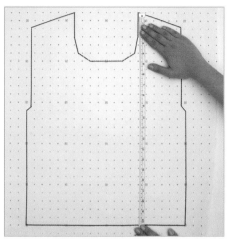

2 Now measure the length of the pattern, toile or garment from hem to shoulder. If you want to save on fabric, halve this measurement.

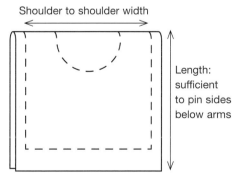

Shoulder to shoulder width

Length: sufficient to pin sides below arms

3 Fold a piece of jersey or appropriate fabric in half. The fold will represent your shoulder seam. Iron the fold. Using pins or a pen, mark on the fabric the width – shoulder to shoulder – on the fold. The length need only be sufficient to pin the sides below the arms. Cut out the tabard, which should be a rectangle shape, or shorter if you are saving fabric.

4 You can now use a pen or pins to mark out a desired neckline. You will need to consider the width and depth of your neckline as well as the shape.

5 Place the tabard over your head and pin at the sides. You can now see your mock neckline and decide if it is right for you. Now adapt the paper pattern; see page 68.

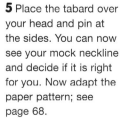

Necklines: Adapting the paper pattern

How to transfer an altered neckline to the paper pattern.

The paper pattern is an easy-to-store tool that can be used again and again to help with sizing and design reference. Here, you will be shown how to alter a paper pattern using the neckline that was designed on the toile (see pages 66–67). You will also learn how to change the neckline to give it a deeper or wider shape, or for a neater fit.

You will need

• Paper pattern (see pages 36–37)
• Spot-and-cross or plain paper
• Sharp scissors
• Glue
• Measurements taken from your preferred neckline (see page 66)
• Ruler
• Pen
• Skirt curve

Getting started

Lay out your pattern on a clean, flat surface with plenty of room to move it around. You can, of course, trace off existing patterns and draw in new necklines to create a new pattern, but small sections of patterns can be changed easily if marked clearly. You may want to use a code, for example, curved neckline marked in blue, V-neck marked in red.

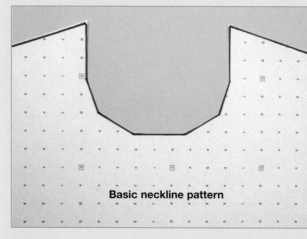

Basic neckline pattern

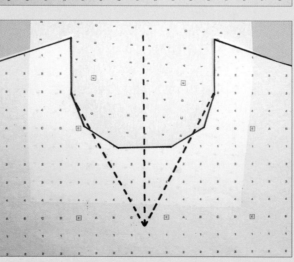

Adding paper

Sometimes you need to add extra paper when adapting a paper pattern. For example, we want to change the neckline from a curve to a V, so will need to add additional paper. Cut a length of paper and glue it to the back of the pattern to fill the neckline. Using the measurements taken from the new neckline, mark the new pattern and draw in the new neckline.

SEE ALSO
Making a paper pattern
Making a paper pattern by transferring your measurements is detailed on pages 36–37.

Altering the patterns
For advice on marking up changes on a paper pattern, see pages 48–51.

Trims and fastenings
Fastenings can add interesting design details at the neck. See pages 114–115 for inspiration.

Changing the neckline to a deeper shape

If you want to change your neckline to a deeper shape, such as a low scoop or deep V, you must allow for your body shape. Keep the shoulder measurement the same to stop the altered shape from gaping.

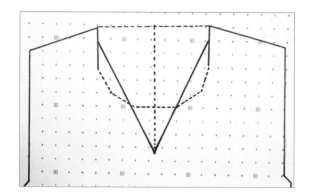

Deep V-neck
Mark the new depth on the pattern at the centre of the neck. Line up a ruler from the shoulder point to the marked depth and draw in the new neckline.

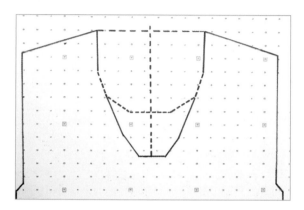

Deep scoop
Mark the new depth on the pattern at the centre of the neck. Mark the flat of the curve at that point (width of centre front neck). Using a ruler or a skirt curve, draw the curve to meet the flat of the existing shoulder point. The new curve will be deeper but will not gape.

Changing the neckline to a wider shape

You may want to change your neckline to a wider shape, such as a boat neck, square or envelope. In all of these designs, it is essential that you keep enough width at the shoulder to prevent the garment from slipping. Type of sleeve will also affect the neckline; a long puff sleeve is heavy and will pull on a wide neck.

When deciding on the width of a neckline, it is especially useful to make up a toile or use the tabard method (see pages 66–67).

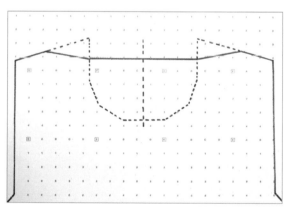

Boat neck
Mark the shoulder width points on the pattern. As a general guide, always leave at least 5cm (2in) for the shoulder width. Mark the depth of the neck at the centre of the pattern and, using a skirt curve for a curve or ruler for straight lines, line up the marked points and draw in the new neckline.

Changing the neckline for a neater fit

When changing a neckline to a neater fit, always consider the head size. If you want a funnel or polo neck to fit snugly, you must introduce some stretch by using a ribbed stitch, or allow for an opening of some sort, which will require a fastening.

Zips can be difficult to use on knitted garments, and can be uncomfortable on a close-fitting neck; some good alternatives include buttons, hooks and eyes or knitted ties (see pages 114–115).

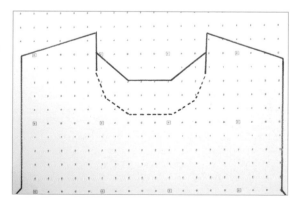

Neater fit
Mark the shoulder width points on the pattern. Mark the depth of the neck at the centre of the pattern and, using a skirt curve for a curve or ruler for straight lines, line up the marked points and draw in the new neckline. If an opening is required, mark this on the pattern.

Necklines: Adapting the written pattern

Transferring the neckline changes from the paper pattern to the written pattern.

Continuing from the previous section, where you adapted the neckline on the paper pattern, you will now be shown how to change your written pattern. It is not necessary to rewrite the whole pattern.

You will need
- Paper pattern marked with necessary neckline alterations
- Written pattern (see pages 52–57)
- Tension swatch in correct yarn (see page 20)
- Tape measure
- Calculator
- Paper and pencil

Finding the first row

First, you will need to know on what row to start shaping the neckline.

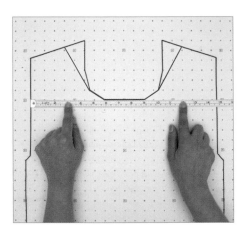

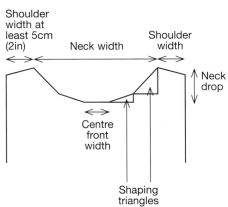

Shoulder width at least 5cm (2in)

Neck width

Shoulder width

Neck drop

Centre front width

Shaping triangles

Wider shape

If you have changed the shape – width – of the neckline but not the depth, the shaping will start on the same row. Re-measure the width of the neck and shoulders and recalculate the shaping using the triangle method (see page 38).

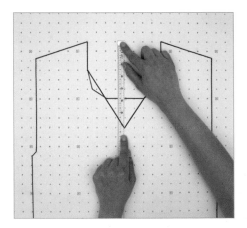

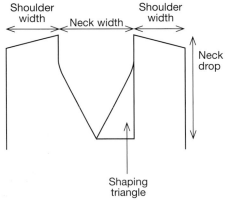

Shoulder width

Neck width

Shoulder width

Neck drop

Shaping triangle

Deeper shape

If you have dropped the neckline, perhaps making the V-neck or scoop deeper, you will start shaping the neckline at an earlier row. To work out this alteration, you need to know the new measurement of the front neck drop. Use your tension swatch to convert the front neck drop measurement to a number of rows. Subtract this number from the total amount of rows to find the row you will start shaping on. Recalculate the shaping as on page 38.

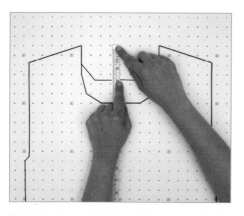

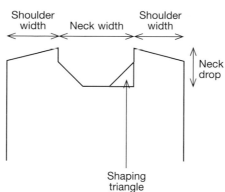

Neater fit

If you have changed the neckline to a neater, more fitted style, you will start the shaping on a later row. To work out this calculation, follow the instructions for a deeper shape (left).

Neckline shaping

To work out the shaping for your new neckline, follow the instructions on pages 38–41. Remember that you will have to square your neckline off to be able to work out the decreases needed in stitches and rows, as shown on page 40.

Alter the written pattern from the new start row, changing the shaping instructions as required.

Front neck drop

From toile straight to written pattern

If you are confident in your sizing and design choices, you may want to go straight to this stage, skipping the paper pattern stage, and make the adaptation directly to your written knitting pattern.

Back neck drop

Back neckline shaping

You can shape the back neck edge as well as the front – this is often done with wide or deep front necklines. Simply decide on the depth of the back neck drop required, and calculate the back neck shaping in the same way as on page 40.

SEE ALSO
Converting the measurements
For more details on how to convert measurements into stitches and rows in a written pattern, see pages 34–35.

Calculating shaping
Further information on how to write shaping into a written pattern can be found on pages 38–41.

Rewriting the instructions
Instructions on how to take measurements from a paper pattern and convert them into a written knitting pattern are given on pages 52–57.

Design details:
Necklines

This section features some interesting design details
that will inspire your choice of neckline.

When picking a neckline, you must consider the type of yarn that the
garment will be knitted in. A cowl neck knitted in a floppy rayon yarn
will look remarkably different to one in a super-chunky wool mix. The
following examples feature a variety of necklines with design details
interpreted in various yarns to create exciting and inspirational
effects, with each neckline designed to demonstrate a different finish
or way of knitting. Refer to the flat pattern below the picture for
technical details.

Necklines can either be knitted
integrally or grafted in place. Details
can enhance the design, such as a
row of purl stitches following the
shaping, or tipping an edge with a
contrasting yarn. Some garments
benefit from being knitted in a different
direction, for example, where the cast-
on edge is the side seam. Note: The
words in **bold grey text** are the actual
pattern instructions.

*The designer has created an original
garment by combining an unusual
neckline with embellishment. The
asymmetric design draws attention to the
neckline, which incorporates an integrated
collar. This is highlighted by the use of a
ribbed stitch.*

SEE ALSO
Constructing the garment
Turn to pages 58–61 to learn how
to join knitted pieces together.

Trims and fastenings
A selection of trims is illustrated
on pages 114–115.

Yo (yarn over)
Page 132.

Picking up stitches
Page 134.

Polo neck crew

This polo neck has been knitted in
stocking stitch in a contrasting colour,
and the cast-off edge creates a gentle
rolled effect.

Polo neck crew: Instructions

Join one shoulder seam.
With right side facing, pick up and knit (see
page 134) enough sts around the neckline to
fit easily over the head.
Work in stocking stitch (beginning P row) for
about 5cm (2in) or to length required.
Cast off loosely.
Join seam and remaining shoulder seam.
Neckband will naturally roll with P
side outwards.
Note: Photo shows an example with stitches
picked up from wrong side of work, creating an
interesting effect at the join.

Cowl neck

This cowl neck has been knitted with a chunky yarn. The resulting scarf effect gives an impression of warmth and could be used on an outer garment.

Raw-edge neck

This neckline has been left with a raw edge, and the shaping around it is highlighted by working full-fashioned shaping. The garment has been knitted sideways from cuff to cuff to highlight the stitch detail.

Frill neck

In this example a frill has been used to create a dramatic garment, with yarns of different weights adding interest.

Cowl neck: Instructions

Join shoulder seams and use a circular needle to pick up and knit (see page 134) sts all around neck edge.

Work in rounds of stocking stitch, increasing at 4 'shaping points', every 4 rows (or as required). Cast off loosely and allow to form a roll.

Raw-edge neck: Instructions

The method of shaping a sideways-knitted neckline is shown in the diagram. There are no shoulder seams. If the shaping is worked a few sts in from the edges (see page 131), the neck edge can be left with no further finishing.

Frill neck: Instructions

Cast on enough stitches to match the length around the neck edge.

Row 1: K1, *yo, K1, repeat from * to end.
Row 2: P.
Row 3: K1, *yo, K2, repeat from * to end.
Row 4: P.
Row 5: K1, *yo, K3, repeat from * to end.
Row 6: P.

Continue in this way to depth required. Change to another colour if desired. Knit 2 rows. Cast off loosely. Sew to neck edge with a firm stitch, otherwise the weight of the frill may drag on the neckline.

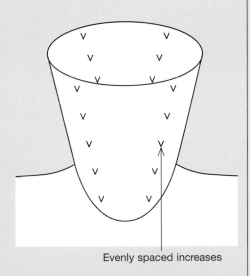

Evenly spaced increases

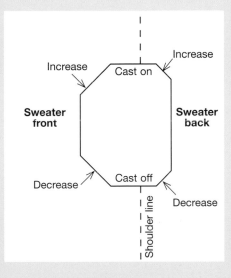

Increase   Increase

Cast on

Sweater front   **Sweater back**

Decrease   Cast off

Shoulder line   Decrease

Shaping shoulders

When shaping the neck, you should also consider the shaping of the shoulders.

Shaping the shoulders of a garment improves the fit of a set-in or dropped armhole, and helps a close-fitting neckline to sit neatly. Shoulder shaping often coincides with the neckline shaping, or follows immediately after it.

When shaping a shoulder, the neck corner usually needs to be just a few rows higher than the top of the armhole (shoulder point). This height difference can be determined by measuring the total length required at the centre back neck, and subtracting the total length required at the outer shoulder point, or by fitting a toile (see page 42) and altering your paper pattern accordingly. Convert the height difference into an even number of rows. Wide necklines with small shoulder seams (about 5cm [2in]) generally do not require any shoulder shaping.

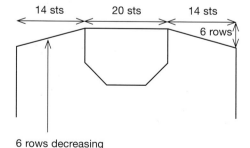

6 rows decreasing
14 sts at each side

In this example each shoulder is 14 stitches wide, and the difference in length between the centre back neck and the outer shoulder point has been converted to 6 rows.

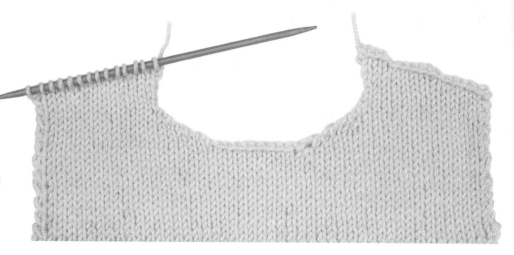

Shaping shoulders on the back

Work to the shoulder point, ending with a wrong side row.

On the back of the sweater in the diagram, 14 stitches must be decreased at each side over 6 rows. There are two ways to do this:

Method 1: Casting off

This method makes a firm shoulder edge that will keep its shape and not stretch, even when used with a full, heavy sleeve. Cast off a group of stitches at the beginning of every row for 6 rows. This will make 3 steps (one half of 6) on each side. So the 14 stitches at each side must be divided into 3 groups: in this case, 2 groups of 5 stitches, and 1 group of 4 stitches. The instructions will read:
Cast off 5 sts at beginning next 4 rows.
Cast off 4 sts at beginning following 2 rows.
Cast off remaining 20 sts (or slip them to a spare needle or stitch holder).
When working in stocking stitch, stitches on wrong side rows may be cast off purlwise, that is, instead of knitting each stitch before casting it off, it can be purled. This makes a smooth edge.

Tip

For a smoother top edge with less obvious steps, on the third and following cast-off rows, slip the first stitch instead of knitting (or purling) it.

On this garment front, the shoulder edge on the right is worked by Method 1 (casting off), and that on the left by Method 2 (short rows).

Note: The words in **bold grey text** are the actual pattern instructions.

Method 2: Short rows

This method makes a more flexible shoulder with a less visible seam line that will drape smoothly over the shoulder.

The calculations are the same, but instead of casting off, the groups of stitches are left unworked, then slipped to a spare needle for the shoulder seams to be joined (page 135). Alternatively, you could use a three-needle cast off to create the seam.

You will need a spare needle for each shoulder, plus a third for the back neck stitches (double-pointed needles are useful, but if you want to put the work aside for a time, a circular needle will hold all the stitches more securely).
1st shoulder row: work to the last 5 sts, turn.
2nd row: sl 1, work to last 5 sts, turn.
3rd and 4th rows: sl 1, work to last 10 sts, turn.
5th and 6th rows: sl 1, work to last 14 sts, turn.
Slip remaining 20 sts to a spare needle for neckline. Slip 14 sts at each shoulder to spare needles for grafting.

Shaping shoulders on the front

On the front of the sweater, each shoulder is worked separately.

Method 1: Casting off

First side

After completing the neck shaping on the first side (see page 38), work to the shoulder point, ending on a WS row.
Cast off 5 sts at beginning next row, work to end. Work 1 row.
Repeat these 2 rows once more.
Cast off remaining 4 sts.
(5 rows worked.)

Second side

After completing the neck shaping, work to the shoulder point to match first side.
Work 1 right side row.
Complete as for first side.
(6 rows worked.)
The shoulder seams should then be joined with a firm seam (see page 135).

Method 2: Short rows

First side

After completing the neck shaping on the first side, work to the shoulder point, ending on a WS row.
Work 1 RS row.
2nd row: work to last 5 sts, turn.
3rd row: sl 1, work to end.
4th row: work to last 10 sts, turn.
5th row: sl 1, work to end.
(5 rows worked.)
Slip 14 sts to a spare needle.

Second side

After completing the neck shaping, work to the shoulder point to match first side, ending on a WS row.
Work 2nd–5th rows as first side.
(4 rows worked.)
Slip 14 sts to a spare needle.
The shoulder seams should then be joined by the grafting method (page 135), when they will be as elastic as a knitted row.

Tip

In the example given, the neckline shaping is complete before the shoulder shaping begins, but sometimes they may coincide. In such cases, it is often a good idea to draw out the shaping on graph paper.

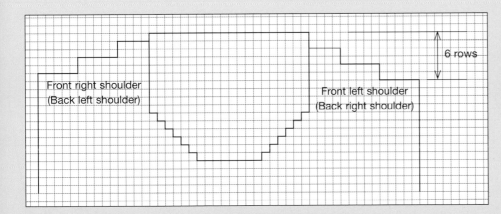

Front right shoulder (Back left shoulder)

Front left shoulder (Back right shoulder)

6 rows

This graph represents the shoulder shaping of the back and front above, with right side of both pieces facing, worked by Method 1.

Balancing the shoulders

Using Method 1, you will see that on the back, the left shoulder shaping (as worn) begins one row above the right shoulder shaping. This is balanced out by the front, where the right shoulder shaping begins one row above the left. So both shoulders will be the same total depth after seaming.

Conversely, if using Method 2, the right shoulder shaping on the back begins one row above that on the left. This is, again, balanced out by the shaping on the front.

CHANGING SLEEVES

Choosing a sleeve design for your garment can be as simple as changing the length, or as complex as changing the shape, length, width and the way it is attached to the body. Either way, it is important that it works with the rest of the garment, and suits the purpose of the piece you are making.

The designer of this catwalk piece has chosen to use an exaggerated bishop sleeve on this dramatic garment. The knitted fabric gathers elegantly at the wrist, and works well with the choice of lightweight yarn.

Design options: Sleeves

As well as their practical use, sleeves can add interest to a garment, so consider your options carefully.

Here is a variety of sleeve types that you may want to use when adapting your pattern. When making your choice, try to achieve a balance in your design. If you have a complicated neckline, use a simple sleeve, and when using a highly designed sleeve, pick a simple neckline. Aim to use elements that contrast and complement each other rather than fight for attention.

Choosing the right length

When adapting your pattern, you have access to a variety of sleeve lengths, including a very short cap sleeve; short sleeve; to the elbow; bracelet or full length. When making your choice, you should consider how and when the garment will be worn, and what yarn it will be knitted in. For instance, a cap sleeve would normally be knitted in a lightweight yarn.

Choosing the right shape

The overall silhouette (or shape) of the garment will be affected by the choice of sleeve. Consider not only the length, but also the sleeve cap and cuff. Possible sleeve shapes include set in; raglan; raglan with yoke; dropped shoulder; cap; bell; leg of mutton; puffed and batwing.

The shape of the sleeve is often determined by how the cuff is designed. Some possibilities for the cuff include rib; ruffle; turn up; drawstring; elasticized; stitch detail or roll edge.

Set in

This classic shape sits neatly on the shoulder and may be a short or long sleeve. It is a simple shape to translate into the knitted stitch, having an easy-to-work sleeve cap and armhole. Often used in lightweight or cashmere garments, the simplicity can be highlighted with full-fashioned shaping or with a contrast stitch at the seams to add design interest. This shape is good for the novice knitter, or for a garment with a complicated neckline.

Cap

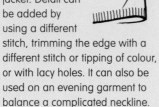

This neat short sleeve works well for a summer garment, or on a top designed to be worn under a jacket. Detail can be added by using a different stitch, trimming the edge with a different stitch or tipping of colour, or with lacy holes. It can also be used on an evening garment to balance a complicated neckline.

Batwing

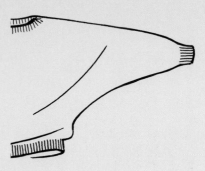

A classic shape that works well for both day and evening styles, this sleeve is knitted integrally with the body; some interesting effects can be achieved by knitting sideways from cuff to cuff. The sleeve is normally finished with a ribbed cuff to control the fullness.

Raglan/full length

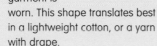

The raglan sleeve sits into a slanted armhole, and is a good sleeve to use when practising decreasing. Often used in casual sportswear-inspired garments, the sleeve allows for ease of movement and works well in both a fitted and loose garment. The top of a raglan sleeve may be shaped to form part of the neckline – right and left sleeves will be mirror images of each other.

Bell

This interesting sleeve shape has a very distinctive look, and the excess of fabric will gently swing when the garment is worn. This shape translates best in a lightweight cotton, or a yarn with drape.

Dropped shoulder

This sleeve shape is very relaxed and can be interpreted in a number of ways. It works well in both a full and short length. It can be knitted in all types of yarn, and when worked in a rayon or fancy yarn, the sleeve will drape elegantly, whereas in wool or cotton the sleeve will have a casual, easy-to-wear look.

Leg of mutton/long ribbed cuff

This distinctive sleeve can be easily interpreted into knit by extending the rib from the cuff up to the elbow, then using plain knit to complete the sleeve cap. You will need to consider how much ease will go into the armhole.

SEE ALSO
Design details: Sleeves
See pages 84–87 for knitted examples of various sleeve types.

Sleeves: Adapting the toile

How to correctly adapt the sleeve on your toile.

In Making and fitting a toile (pages 42–45), you were shown how to ease the sleeve into an adapted body shape. You will now learn how to adapt the sleeve cap and the armhole. With the skills learnt in this section, you will be able to change, adapt and substitute sleeves onto existing toiles.

You will need
- Toile (see pages 42–45)
- Tape measure
- Pen
- Sharp scissors
- Pins
- Spare fabric
- Sewing machine or needle and thread
- Iron and ironing board

Length of sleeve, width of sleeve and width at shoulder are the areas you may want to change on your toile. Changing length or width at the bottom of the sleeve (in the area between the cuff and the armhole) does not affect the armhole shaping on the body. Changes in measurements to the sleeve cap (above the armhole) may necessitate a change to the armhole shaping. In the examples shown here, the sleeves are eased in to avoid changing body shapes (see page 49).

Getting started

Try on the toile and decide on the changes you would like to make. Use pins to adjust the fit. When happy with the fit, turn the toile inside out and re-pin or mark the alteration on the inside. Keep a note of the measurements that you are altering since you will need these to alter the paper pattern.

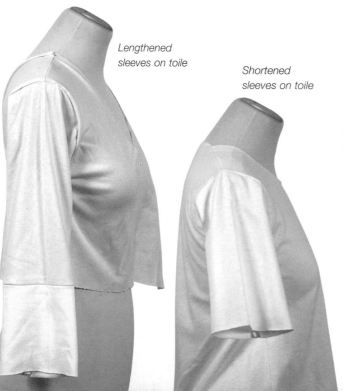

Lengthened sleeves on toile

Shortened sleeves on toile

Adjusting length

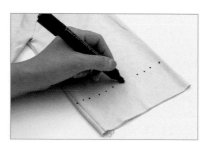

To shorten sleeves
1 While wearing the toile, measure from the shoulder point to the desired length of the cuff. Remove the toile and lay it flat, then note the position of the new shoulder length.

2 Use a pen to mark the desired length on the toile and cut the cuff to the mark.

To lengthen sleeves
1 Wear the toile and measure from the shoulder point to the desired cuff. Make a note of the complete measurement, or of the extra length required. Either cut a new sleeve to the desired length and replace the whole sleeve, or cut an additional piece of fabric to size and join this to the existing cuff. Sew the additional piece to the existing cuff and press the seam open.

2 Turn the sleeve right-side out to check the extended length.

Adjusting width

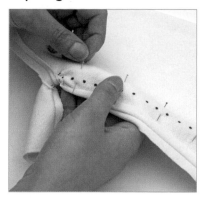

Decreasing the width
While wearing the toile, pin the cuff at the seam to adjust it to the desired width. Take the toile off and measure the width to be decreased. The angle of the seam will be changed to meet the armhole. Lay the toile flat. Mark the adjusted width in from the existing seam, and pin. Sew the new seam, unpin and press the new seam open. If you are happy with the alteration, cut away the excess fabric.

Increasing the width
1 If you are making only a minor adjustment, you may be able to rework the sleeve by using the seam allowance as excess fabric. If, however, a larger adjustment is needed below the armhole point, you will need to cut a new sleeve, or add an insert as shown in step 2.

2 Unpick the sleeve at the seam. Cut an insert to increase the sleeve to the desired width. Pin in place, sew the seams and press open. Turn the garment right-side out and try the adjusted sleeve. This insert will need to be added to your paper pattern (see pages 80–81). Any adjustments should now be transferred to your paper pattern, as shown on the next page.

Adjusting width at shoulder
Pin the toile so that the sleeve fits comfortably on the shoulder. If the fit is not correct, you will need to decide whether the sleeve is causing the problem or if it is the shoulder width on the body that needs adjusting.

To alter the sleeve
Mark the adjustment needed on the sleeve, then unpick the sleeve and press. Cut the sleeve to the adjusted amount, then pin and re-sew to the body.

To alter the body
Unpick the sleeve and re-cut the shoulder width, then re-pin and re-sew the sleeve to the adjusted body.

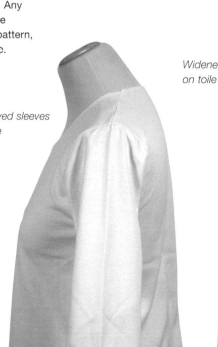

Narrowed sleeves on toile

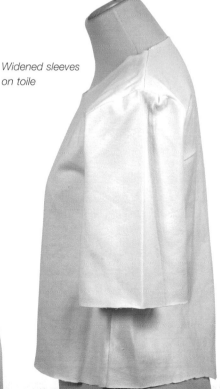

Widened sleeves on toile

SEE ALSO
Making and fitting a toile
Detailed instructions on how to make a toile can be found on pages 42–45.

How to alter a toile
Learn how to adjust a toile for a perfect fit on pages 46–47.

Sleeves: Adapting the paper pattern

Transferring the changes made to the toile to the paper pattern.

The sleeve alterations now need to be transferred to the paper pattern. These may include the length of the sleeve, width of the sleeve and the width at the shoulder.

You will need

- Paper pattern (see pages 36–37)
- Tape measure
- Notes on the alterations to be made
- Spot-and-cross or plain paper
- Glue
- Ruler
- Pattern master
- Pen
- Sharp scissors

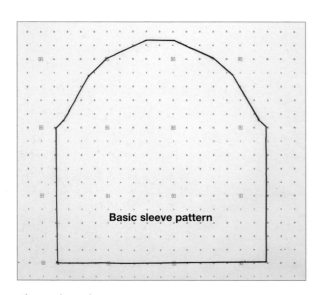

Basic sleeve pattern

Getting started

Lay out your pattern on a clean, flat surface with plenty of room to move it around. If you are adjusting a pattern that you want to keep, you could mark the alterations in a different colour. If you are using a rib at the cuff, remember to mark it on the sleeve pattern. The ribbed area should be drawn in straight because the rib will naturally pull in. Start any sleeve shaping on the first row of plain knitting after the rib.

Sleeve length

Use a ruler to mark the new length on the pattern. You could also cut away the excess pattern paper, but this is not essential. The excess pattern can then be cut away or ignored.

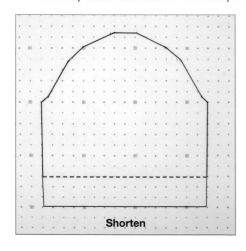

Shorten

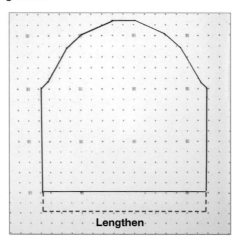

Lengthen

Altering the sleeve length

Lay the existing sleeve pattern flat and measure from the sleeve cap to the cuff. Mark the paper pattern at the adjusted length. If you are lengthening the sleeve, you may need to add additional paper to the pattern by gluing it to the reverse. Line up a ruler at the new length and draw in a straight line.

Sleeve width

Use a ruler to mark the alteration; this will change the amount of stitches to be increased to the armhole point.

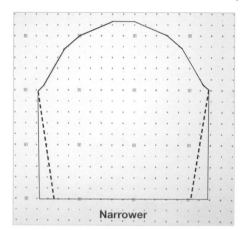

Narrower

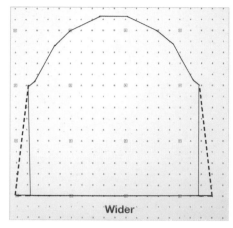

Wider

Altering the sleeve width

Lay the paper pattern flat and mark the alteration at the cuff. If you are widening the sleeve, you may need to add additional paper to the pattern by gluing it to the reverse. Use a ruler to draw a line from the adjusted mark to the underarm point; this will change the shaping between the hem and the armhole point.

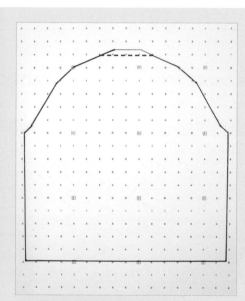

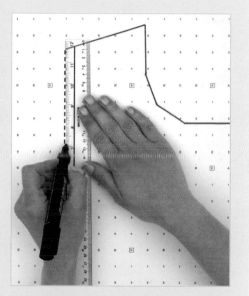

SEE ALSO
Making a paper pattern
Making a paper pattern by transferring your measurements is detailed on pages 36–37.

Altering the patterns
For advice on marking up changes on a paper pattern, see pages 48–51.

Altering the sleeve width at the shoulder

To make an adjustment to the sleeve, mark the alteration at the sleeve cap and use a ruler to fill in the adjustment equally around the sleeve cap. Cut away or ignore the existing pattern.

Altering the shoulder width on the body

In this case you will be making an adjustment to the armhole and shoulder point. Mark the alteration at the shoulder. Using a ruler, follow the line down to meet the armhole, and mark the adjustment. Cut away or ignore the existing pattern.

Sleeves: Adapting the written pattern

After adapting the paper pattern, you can make changes to your written knitting pattern.

Begin by identifying where the alterations will take place and marking these positions on your paper pattern.

It can help to convert all of your measurements into rows and stitches before you start to write the pattern (use the table on page 33 to help you – don't forget to round the figures up or down to even numbers). To speed up the pattern-writing process you can write the pattern but leave blanks to drop in your rows and stitches.

You will need

- Tension swatch in correct yarn (see page 20)
- Paper pattern marked with necessary sleeve alterations
- Written pattern (see pages 52–57)
- Tape measure
- Calculator
- Paper and pencil

Note: The words in **bold grey text** are the actual pattern instructions.

Sample pattern

This is the basic sleeve pattern on which the adaptations that follow are based.

The instructions for this sleeve would read:
Cast on 42 stitches.
14 rows are required to underarm, increasing 2 sts at each side.
To spread the increases evenly, work them on rows 5 and 11:
Inc 1 st at each end 5th and 11th rows. Work 3 rows. 46 sts. 14 rows.
To shape the sleeve cap, we need to decrease 19 sts at each side over 22 rows. Therefore, there will be 22 – 19 = 3 rows without any shaping. Space the unshaped rows evenly, for example on the 6th, 12th, and 18th rows:
Dec 1 st at each end next 5 rows. Work 1 row without shaping.
Repeat these 6 rows twice more. 16 sts remain.
Dec 1 st at each end next 4 rows. (22 sleeve cap rows complete.)
Cast off remaining 8 sts.

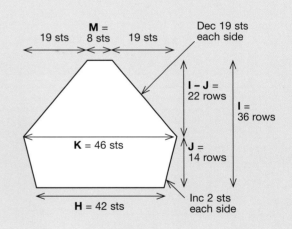

M = 8 sts
19 sts — 19 sts
Dec 19 sts each side
I – J = 22 rows
I = 36 rows
K = 46 sts
J = 14 rows
H = 42 sts
Inc 2 sts each side

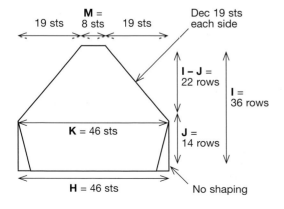

M = 8 sts
19 sts — 19 sts
Dec 19 sts each side
I – J = 22 rows
I = 36 rows
K = 46 sts
J = 14 rows
H = 46 sts
No shaping

Wider sleeve

This sleeve has been widened at the lower edge by adding 2 sts at each side to the cast-on.
The amended instructions begin:
Cast on 46 sts.
There is no shaping between the cast-on edge and the underarm:
Work 14 rows.
The sleeve cap is then shaped in the same way as for the sample pattern, above.

SEE ALSO
Converting the measurements
For more details on how to convert measurements into rows in a written pattern, see pages 34–35.

Calculating shaping
More information on how to write shaping into a written pattern can be found on pages 38–41.

Rewriting the instructions
Instructions on how to take measurements from a paper pattern and convert them into a written knitting pattern are given on pages 52–57.

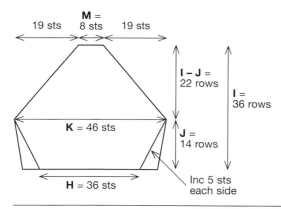

Narrower sleeve

This sleeve is made narrower at the lower edge by casting on fewer stitches, therefore more stitches must be increased between the lower edge and the underarm to achieve the correct underarm width.
The amended instructions read:
Cast on 36 sts.
14 rows are required to underarm, increasing 5 sts at each side.

14 divided by 5 = approx. 3, so increasing should take place on every 3rd row, but we need to squeeze the last pair of increases in on the 14th row:
Increase 1 st at each end 3rd, 6th, 9th, 12th and 14th rows. 46 sts.
The sleeve cap is then shaped in the same way as for the sample pattern, opposite.

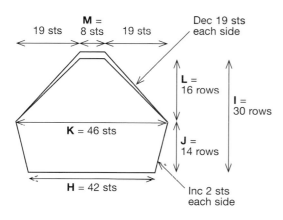

Amend the sleeve cap

Here, the sleeve cap is 6 rows shorter than the sample pattern: 19 sts must therefore be decreased at each side over 16 rows (instead of 22 rows).
To shape the sleeve cap, we need to decrease 19 sts at each side over 16 rows. Therefore, there will be 19 – 16 = 3 rows on which 2 sts will be decreased at each end (and therefore 13 rows with 1 st decreased at each end). To space the double

decrease rows evenly throughout the sleeve cap:
Dec 1 st at each end next 4 rows.
Dec 2 sts at each end next row.
34 sts remain.
Repeat these 5 rows twice more.
10 sts remain.
Dec 1 st at each end next row.
16 sleeve cap rows complete.
Cast off remaining 8 sts.

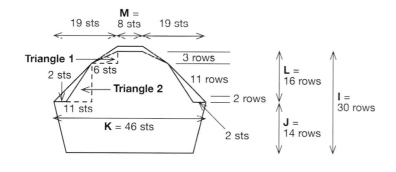

Curved sleeve cap

After altering your toile and paper pattern, you may find that a curved sleeve cap is required for the fit you want to achieve. This example shows a typical set-in sleeve cap, which might be shaped as follows:

Shape sleeve cap
At the beginning of the sleeve cap shaping, the outline at each side is almost horizontal. This may be achieved by casting off a small group of stitches at each side, at the beginning of the first two rows.
Cast off 2 sts at beginning next 2 rows. 42 sts remain.
These 2 rows must be counted as part of the 16 sleeve cap rows, so 14 rows remain for the rest of the shaping. You can calculate the shaping of the curves by the triangle method, as shown on page 38. In our example, triangle 1 calculates to 11 sts wide and 11 rows deep:
Decrease 1 st at each end of every row for 11 rows.
20 sts remain.
13 sleeve cap rows complete.
Triangle 2 calculates to 6 sts wide and 3 rows deep.
Decrease 2 sts at each end of every row for 3 rows.
16 sleeve cap rows complete.
Cast off remaining 8 sts.

Design details: Sleeves

Now that you have all the skills required to adjust your sleeve pattern, take a look at these interesting sleeve shapes and cuff details to help inspire your designs.

When choosing a sleeve shape, you must consider what effect it will have on the overall silhouette of the garment. Will it complement the neckline, and is it suited to the type of yarn? Each sleeve shown here has been chosen to demonstrate different qualities. Refer to the flat pattern below the image for more details. Use the triangle method (see page 38) to calculate shaping.

As with necklines, small details can add design interest, and the sleeve cap and cuff can benefit from special attention. Consider full-fashioned shaping or stitch contrast around the shaping on the sleeve cap, while cuffs can be tipped with a different colour or contrast yarn. Various fastenings, such as buttons or ties, can be used to personalize a garment.

Note: The words in **bold grey text** are the actual pattern instructions.

SEE ALSO
Design details: Necklines
Necklines and sleeves need to work together and not compete for attention. See pages 72–73 for some ideas.

Trims and fastenings
You might like to add buttons or ties to sleeve cuffs. See pages 114–115 for inspiration.

Cap sleeve

This small sleeve can be used on many garments. It can vary in length from hardly there to just below the armhole. Note that the decreasing has been highlighted by full-fashioned shaping three stitches from the edge.

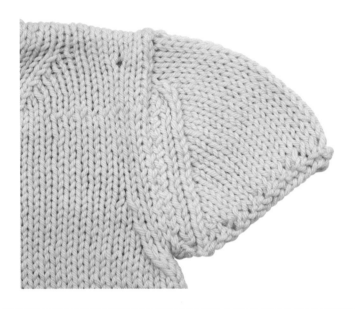

Cap sleeve: Sample instructions

At underarm:
Shape sleeve cap
To decrease 7 sts at each side over 14 rows:
**Decrease 1 st at each end on 1st, 3rd, 5th, 7th, 9th, 11th and 13th rows.
26 sts remain. (Work 14th row.)**
To decrease 6 sts at each side over 6 rows:
**Decrease 1 st at each end on next 6 rows. 14 sts remain.
Cast off or slip remaining sts to a stitch holder.**

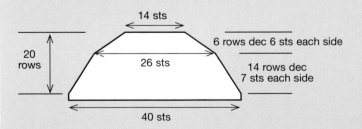

14 sts

6 rows dec 6 sts each side

20 rows

26 sts

14 rows dec 7 sts each side

40 sts

Cap sleeve with a puff

This cap sleeve has been knitted larger than the armhole and then eased in, resulting in a slight puff at the shoulder point. Because there is extra fabric in the sleeve cap, a lightweight woollen yarn has been used.

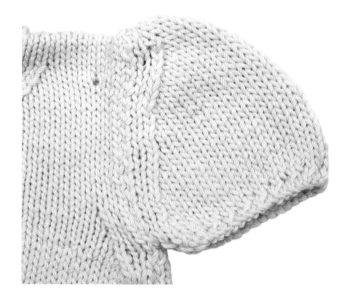

Raglan sleeve

The top edge of a raglan sleeve forms part of the neckline, and may be shaped as shown on the diagram below. This neck edge shaping is reversed for left and right sleeves. This sleeve has been knitted in a lacy stitch to highlight the shaping. Both pieces have been knitted with full-fashioned shaping (see page 131) to add interest to the seam.

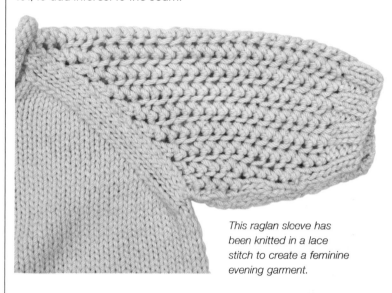

This raglan sleeve has been knitted in a lace stitch to create a feminine evening garment.

Cap sleeve with a puff: Sample instructions

At underarm:
Shape sleeve cap
To decrease 5 sts at each side over 20 rows:
Decrease 1 st at each end on 1st, 5th, 9th, 13th and 17th rows.
30 sts remain. (Work 18th–20th rows.)
To decrease 6 sts at each side over 6 rows:
Decrease 1 st at each end next 6 rows. 18 sts remain.
Cast off or slip remaining sts onto a stitch holder.

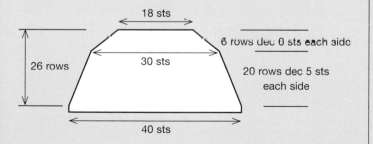

Raglan sleeve: Sample instructions

At underarm:
Shape raglan sleeve cap
To decrease 4 sts at each side over 4 rows:
Decrease 1 st at each end next 4 rows. 34 sts remain.
To decrease 13 sts at each side over 26 rows:
Decrease 1 st at each end next row, then every other row, 13 times in all. 8 sts remain.
(Work 1 WS row.)
To shape neck edge
For left sleeve (shown in diagram):
Decrease 1 st at beg next row.
work to end. Cast off 2 sts at beg next row.
Repeat last 2 rows once more.
Cast off remaining 2 sts.
For the right sleeve, the neck edge shaping is reversed as follows:
Cast off 2 sts at beg and dec 1 st at end of next row.
Work 1 row.
Repeat last 2 rows once more.
Cast off remaining 2 sts.

Diagram labels (left, cap sleeve):
18 sts
6 rows dec 0 sts each side
30 sts
26 rows
20 rows dec 5 sts each side
40 sts

Diagram labels (right, raglan sleeve):
2 sts
4 rows dec 2 sts at back armhole edge and 4 sts at front armhole edge
8 sts
26 rows dec 13 sts each side
34 sts
4 rows dec 4 sts each side
42 sts
20 rows inc 4 sts each side
34 sts

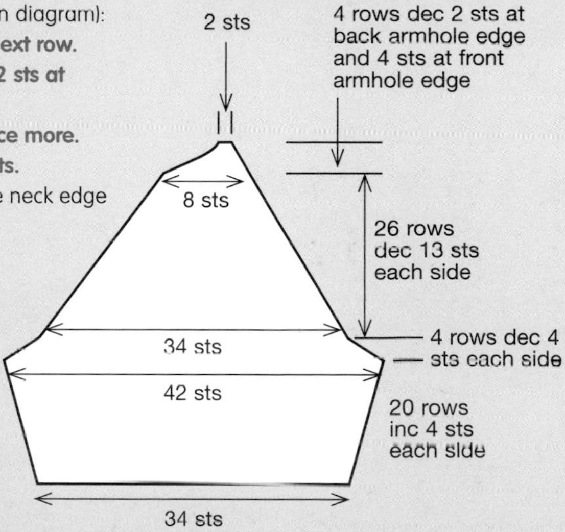

Leg of mutton sleeve

In this example, a three-quarter length leg of mutton sleeve is knitted in a lightweight wool. Extra shaping is added by using rib at the cuff, while the sleeve cap is knitted in a plain stitch. The excess fabric at the sleeve cap is gathered in to the shoulder point to give a slightly puffed shoulder.

Split leg of mutton

Unusually, this sleeve is knitted as a two-piece (a method usually reserved for woven fabrics). Small buttons at the cuff keep the sleeve tight, and the large sleeve cap is eased into the armhole to create small, even puckering.

Leg of mutton sleeve: Sample instructions

Using smaller needles, cast on 30 sts and work 30 rib rows.
Change to larger needles and continue in stocking stitch.
Increase 1 st at each end on 1st and every foll 6th row, 4 times. 38 sts.
Work to 20 rows from rib.
Shape sleeve cap
To decrease 4 sts at each side over 8 rows:
Decrease 1 st at each end next row, then every other row, 4 times.
(Work 1 WS row.) 30 sts remain. Decrease 1 st at each end every row 10 times. 10 sts remain. Cast off.

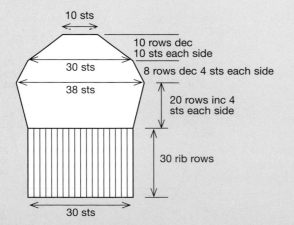

Split leg of mutton: Sample instructions

Left half
Using smaller needles, cast on 16 sts and work 12 rib rows.
Change to larger needles and stocking stitch. Work 18 rows.
Shape sleeve
Increase 1 st at beg next and every foll 6th row, 4 times. 20 sts.
Work to 38 rows from rib.
Shape sleeve cap
To decrease 4 sts over 8 rows:
Decrease 1 st at beg next row then every other row, 4 times. 16 sts remain.
Work 1 WS row.
To decrease 10 sts over 10 rows:
Decrease 1 st at beg next row, and 1 st at end of foll row. Repeat these 2 rows 4 more times. 6 sts remain.
Cast off.
Right half
As left half, reversing all shaping.

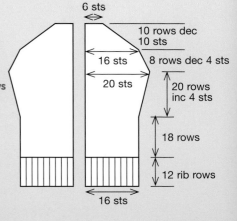

Batwing

This loose shaped sleeve is usually held in place at the cuff by rib stitch. The sleeves are shaped with a gradual increase above the cuff and a sharp increase nearer to the body to achieve the required curve.

In this example the cuff has been used as a cast-on edge so that the stitch detail runs across the body, as opposed to the usual direction. This technique works very well when creating garments that drape, and is worth keeping in mind when knitting large pieces, since it may make the shaping easier to work out.

This garment is knitted with popcorn details to highlight the unusual direction. It is knitted as one piece – it has no shoulder seams, a detail highlighted by the use of pattern.

After knitting the main part sideways from cuff to cuff, the waist is finished by picking up stitches to work ribbing downwards on the front and back waist edges.

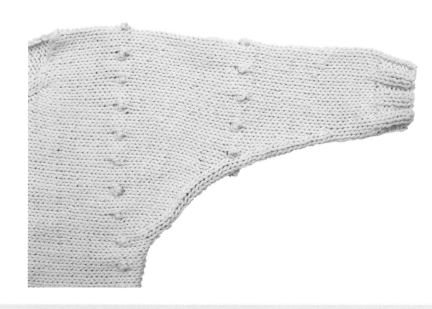

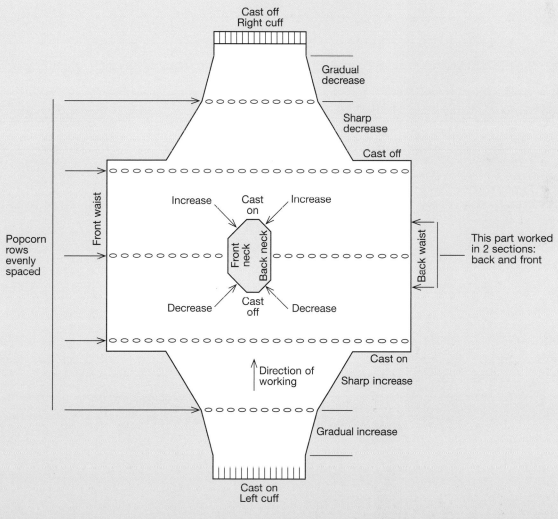

This loose-fit cardigan has been given a body-conscious shape by the addition of a belt. Extended and placed ribs, stitch details and knitted belts tied at the waist can add interest and make a garment more feminine.

CHANGING BODY SHAPES

When creating a knitted garment, fit is a fundamental consideration. The garment will be made to your measurements, but fine-tuning will create different silhouettes.

Design options:
Body shape

The silhouette of a garment is decided by a number of factors that affect its overall shape.

Areas to be considered include the fit of the garment; sleeve shape and length; shoulder shape; neckline; length of garment and seam lines.

Building on the previous sections where you were shown necklines and sleeve shapes, the following pages illustrate a variety of body shapes and how to change the shape of a garment on a toile and paper pattern. It is important to pick a silhouette that suits your body shape. Assess the shape of the clothes in your wardrobe, and decide whether you are happy with the fit. Do they highlight the best parts of your figure? Use these considerations to inform your design choices, while also making sure that all the elements of the garment work together to create the perfect piece of clothing.

Designers often start manipulating the silhouette by exaggerating parts of the body with carefully cut shapes and padding, or by altering seams and dropping waistlines. Designers are also concerned with proportion – how the body is divided by the placement of the waist and seams, placement of details, and placement of colour or pattern.

The fit

Possibly the main consideration of any garment is the fit, since this will affect the overall look. On pages 30–35, you were shown how to take measurements and convert them into a written pattern. You can now be confident that the garment will fit you perfectly; however, you must decide how you would like the garment to look. For example, a T-shirt can be designed in a very body-conscious style, or loose with a drop sleeve.

When choosing the fit of your garment, bear in mind the weight of the yarn you want to use: heavyweight yarns are normally suited to a looser fit, while lightweight yarns can be used for any fit.

Loose fit

This easy-to-wear body shape can be very flattering. Consideration should be paid to sleeve styles: Drop sleeve, raglan and batwing, bell and kimono will work well, but avoid set-in and puff sleeves. A loose fit can vary immensely. Consider the length of the garment, and avoid swamping the body. Consider also the choice of yarn, whether you require drape and whether the fabric will be held in place by a rib or allowed to swing free.

Body conscious

This shape works well in stretch yarns and ribbed knitting. Knitted sportswear and underwear often use Lycra to hug the body and follow muscle contours. Shrunken shapes can flatter the figure, and are often used in cardigans and shrugs. The opposite from loose fit, any slim-fitting sleeve will work well.

Waisted

A garment can be transformed by the placement of the waist. You should consider where the waist would sit on the body, whether you want it to sit naturally, dropped or high. A high waist can be very slimming on a slim-fitting garment, and a dropped waist can look very elegant on a long line. Knitted rib or a belt can be used to pull a garment in at the waist. An alternative method is to fashion the garment with waist shaping.

Long line

Body length will affect the proportions of the garment. Garments can be of any length, but yarn choice, finish and trims all need to work with the garment length to create a balanced design.

Belted

This long line cardigan is given shape by being belted at the waist. Pockets will draw the eye to the upper part of the garment and can add interest to a classic knitted garment.

Ribbed

Rib can be used to alter the body shape and add interest. This design has a rib that stops on different rows to highlight shaping details at the waist. The rib on the cuff of the sleeve has been extended under the arm and meets the extended rib on the body at the underarm.

SEE ALSO
Design details: Body shapes
Turn to pages 94–97 to see knitted examples of body shapes.

Body shape:
Adapting the toile

Adapting the toile is the first step when experimenting with a garment's body shape.

Using the same steps as with necklines and sleeves, you can alter the body shape on the toile, then adapt the paper pattern and written pattern to reflect your changes.

You will need
- Toile (see pages 42–45)
- Pins
- Pen
- Sewing machine or needle and thread
- Iron and ironing board
- Paper pattern (see pages 36–37)
- Written pattern (see pages 52–57)
- Skirt curve
- Spare fabric (optional)

Techniques for effecting changes to the silhouette include pulling in excess fabric with a seam, adding a waist, turning a pullover into a cardigan and adding details such as pockets and a belt.

Changing the body shape
Body width may be decreased at the centre of the body, or by shaping the waist at the side seams. Body width may also be increased in the same places by inserting extra pieces of fabric.

Taking excess fabric from the centre of the body
1 While wearing the toile, pull the excess fabric from the centre of the garment and pin. If you are happy with the fit, remove the toile, lay it on a table and mark on the alteration.

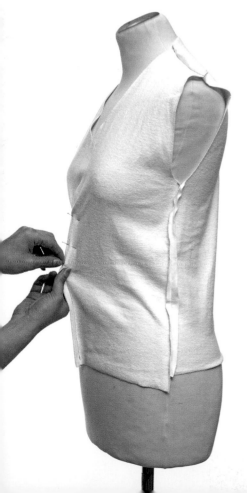

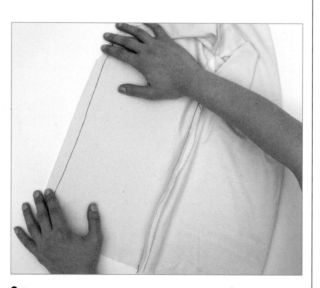

2 Re-sew the toile – you will now have a centre seam. Repeat the process on the back and press the seams. Now alter the paper pattern and written pattern to reflect the changes made to the toile (see pages 92–93 for instructions).

Shaping a waist
1 While wearing the toile, pin it at the waist to the desired fit.

2 Remove the toile and lay it flat, then mark in the largest alteration. Using a skirt curve, draw a curve from the hem to the marked point. Then draw a curve from the marked point to the underarm.

3 You may want to re-pin and check the fit at this stage. If you are happy with the alteration, sew the new seam, cut away the excess fabric and press the seam. Finish by altering the paper and written patterns to reflect the changes made (see pages 96–97 for instructions).

Changing a pullover into a cardigan

Change any pullover into a cardigan by splitting the front into two halves.

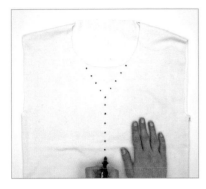

1 Lay the toile flat and mark any adjustments to the front neckline. Find the centre front and mark from the neckline to the hem.

2 Cut through the marked line, to create two parts to the front. Change the paper pattern and written knit pattern to encompass the alterations (see pages 48–51 and 52–57 for instructions). The front will now need to be knitted as two separate pieces. You should also consider how the fronts will fasten (see pages 114–115).

Adding design details

You may want to add a belt or pockets, or change the neckline; these details will affect the body shape.

Belt
Cut a length of fabric and try it on with the toile. Mark on the toile where the belt will sit, considering the length and width of the belt. You will need a paper pattern or measurements to work out a written pattern for the belt.

Collars and cowls
For collars and cowls that are to be grafted to the garment, either mark on the toile or add additional pieces.

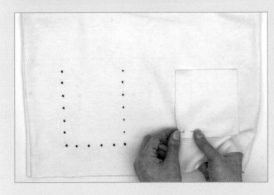

Pockets
Use the appropriate method to alter your toile. The first method is to draw the pocket onto the toile, considering its placement and dimensions. Alternatively, cut the pocket from additional fabric and attach it to the toile. You will need to make a paper pattern of the pocket to be able to calculate the shaping needed when writing the knitting pattern.

SEE ALSO
Making and fitting a toile
Detailed instructions on how to make a toile and then adjust it for the perfect fit can be found on pages 42–45.

Altering the patterns
For advice on marking up changes on a paper pattern, see pages 48–51.

Trims and fastenings
Examples of types of fastening can be found on pages 114–115.

Seams
Turn to page 135 to learn how to join knitted pieces together.

Body shape:
Adapting the written pattern

As in the previous sections, any changes that you make to your toile must be changed on the paper pattern, and then changed on the written pattern.

In the previous section, an example was given on how to adjust the body shape. In this section we will be amending those changes to the written pattern.

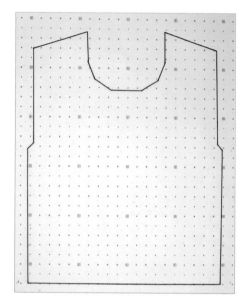

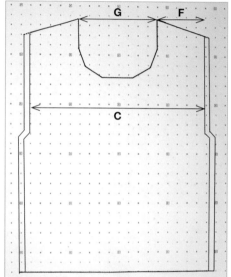

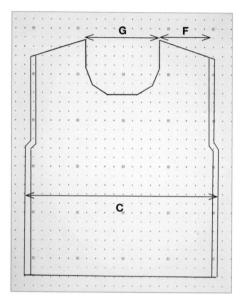

Taking our standard body shape pattern, you will be shown how to adjust for a narrower body, wider body, longer body and shorter body. Shaping a waist is described on pages 96–97.

Note: The words in **bold grey text** are the actual pattern instructions.

Narrower body shape

In this example we will adjust the body shape to decrease the width by 4cm (1½in). You will need to cast on fewer stitches. To calculate this decrease: 4cm x 1.4 (stitches per cm) = 5.6 round up to 6 stitches or 1.5in x 3.5 (stitches per inch) = 5.25, round up to 6 stitches.

The original cast on was 56 stitches. 56 – 6 = 50, so the written pattern would be amended to read **cast on 50 stitches.** The shaping at the armhole will remain the same, but the stitches at the bust measurement C will need to be adjusted. If C = 50 stitches in the original pattern, the new measurement (C) is 50 – 6 = 44 stitches. This in turn will affect the number of stitches for the neck width (G) and shoulder width (F).

Wider body shape

In this example we will adjust the body shape to increase the width by 4cm (1½in). You will need to cast on more stitches. To calculate this increase: 4cm x 1.4 (stitches per cm) = 5.6 round up to 6 stitches or 1.5in x 3.5 (stitches per inch) = 5.25, round up to 6 stitches.

The original cast on was 56 stitches. 56 + 6 = 62, so the new instructions begin **cast on 62 stitches.** The shaping at the armhole will remain the same but the stitches at the bust measurement (C) will need to be adjusted. If C = 50 stitches in the original pattern, the new measurement (C) is 50 + 6 = 56 stitches. Again, this will affect the numbers of stitches for the neck width (G) and shoulder width (F).

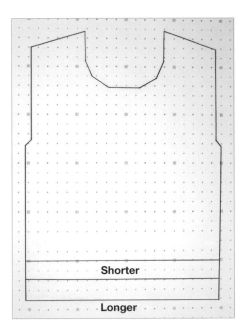

Longer body

For a longer body, work more rows between the hem and the armhole.

Originally, 60 rows were worked from the hem to the armhole. To extend the body length by 3cm (1⅛in), the calculation is: 3cm x 1.8 (rows per cm) = 5.4, round up to 6 rows or 1.2in x 4.5 (rows per inch) = 5.4, round up to 6 rows (it's always a good idea to use even numbers).
60 + 6 = 66 rows
Therefore the amended pattern will read:
Work 66 rows from hem to armhole.

Shorter body

For a shorter body work fewer rows between the hem and the armhole. Originally, 60 rows were worked from the hem to the armhole.
To decrease the body length by 3cm (1⅛in), the calculation is:
3cm x 1.8 (rows per cm) = 5.4, round up to 6 rows or 1.2in x 4.5 (rows per inch) = 5.4, round up to 6 rows (it's always a good idea to use even numbers).
60 − 6 = 54 rows
Therefore the amended pattern will read:
Work 54 rows from hem to armhole.

Body-conscious shape

Most knitted body-conscious garments, such as sportswear or underwear, are machine knitted on a very fine-gauge machine, using yarns blended with elastic or Lycra. However, it is possible to achieve some of these effects with hand knitting.

Some hand-knit yarns contain Lycra or elastic; check the yarn ball band for details. Yarns with these properties will need care when washing since they shrink with heat.

This garment combines a variety of hand-knit techniques to create a body-conscious sweater dress. The designer has explored a variety of yarns in a considered tonal colour palette. Panels have been knitted using a combination of stitches, knitted and seamed in various directions to follow the contours of the body.

Including pattern

You can use your paper pattern to plan stripes or patterns on the sleeve and body. The paper pattern can be used to plot patterns or, as in this example, stripes. Start at the armhole point and mark the pattern from there. You can often match the sleeve to the body pattern from the armhole to the shoulder, but this depends on the sleeve type.

Design details: Body shapes

These two basic body shapes can be adapted in innumerable ways to create the look you want.

Below each example is a sample pattern and a diagram to explain how the design works.

Tip
Groups of stitches are left on stitch holders at the front and back neck to be knitted up later when adding the neckline; if a firmer neck edge is preferred, they may be cast off instead.

Raglan sweater body

Most raglan sweaters are loose fitting as the sleeve lends itself to this shape; the example on the right skims the body and finishes on the hip.

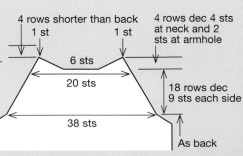

Note: The words in **bold grey text** are the actual pattern instructions.

Back

Using smaller needles, cast on 54 sts. Work 8 rib rows.
Change to larger needles. Continue in stocking stitch throughout.
Work 42 rows.
Shape raglan armholes
To decrease 8 sts at each side over 8 rows:
Decrease 1 st at each end of next 8 rows. 38 sts remain.
To decrease 11 sts at each side over 22 rows:
Decrease 1 st at each end next row. Work 1 row. *
Repeat these 2 rows, 12 more times. 12 sts remain.
Cast off (or slip sts to a stitch holder).

Front

Note that the front neck shaping ends a few rows lower than the back neck (4 rows in our example). If you look at the raglan sleeve pattern on page 85, you will see that the front armhole edge totals 30 rows, while the back armhole edge totals 34 rows, so that adjoining armhole edges match exactly. The shaped top edge of the sleeve forms part of the neck shaping.
Instructions for the front shown in the diagram read:
Work as given for back to *.
Repeat the last 2 rows, 8 more times. 20 sts remain.
Shape front neck: first side
Work 7 sts, decreasing as set at armhole. 6 sts remain. Turn and work on these sts only:
To decrease 3 sts at neck edge and 1 st at armhole over next 3 rows:
Decrease 1 st at neck edge on next row.
Decrease 1 st at each edge on foll row.
Decrease 1 st at neck edge on next row. 2 sts remain.
Work 2 sts tog and fasten off.
Second side
With right side of work facing, slip 6 sts at centre front to a stitch holder and rejoin yarn at right of remaining sts. Complete to match first side reversing shaping.

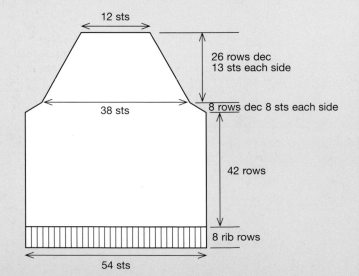

Back diagram labels:
- 12 sts
- 26 rows dec 13 sts each side
- 8 rows dec 8 sts each side
- 38 sts
- 42 rows
- 8 rib rows
- 54 sts

Front diagram labels:
- 4 rows shorter than back
- 1 st
- 1 st
- 4 rows dec 4 sts at neck and 2 sts at armhole
- 6 sts
- 20 sts
- 18 rows dec 9 sts each side
- 38 sts
- As back

Set-in armhole body

The body length of this sweater has been extended to finish just below the hip. The leg-of-mutton sleeves (see page 86) are fitted to the set-in armholes. You could also use cap sleeves (see page 84).

Tip

Instead of casting off the shoulder sts, you can slip them to stitch holders and graft or three-needle cast off the shoulder seams later as described on pages 74–75.

SEE ALSO
Seams
Turn to page 135 to learn how to join knitted pieces together.

Shaping shoulders
This is described in detail on pages 74–75.

Back

Using smaller needles, cast on 54 sts and work 8 rib rows.
Change to larger needles and work in stocking stitch throughout.
Work 40 rows.
Shape set-in armholes
To decrease 3 sts at each side over 4 rows:
Decrease 1 st at each end next 3 rows. Work 1 row. 48 sts remain.
To decrease 2 sts at each side over 8 rows:
Decrease 1 st at each end 3rd and foll 4th row.
Work 1 row. 44 sts remain. *
Work 22 rows.
Shape shoulders
To decrease 12 sts at each side over 6 rows:
Cast off 4 sts at beginning next 6 rows. Slip remaining 20 sts to a stitch holder.

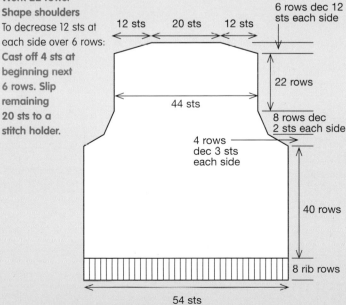

Front

Work as given for back to *.
Work 6 rows.
Shape front neck: first side
Work 17 sts, turn and work on these sts only:
To decrease 5 sts at neck edge over next 11 rows:
Work 1 row.
Decrease 1 st at neck edge on next row.
Repeat these 2 rows, 4 more times. Work 1 row. 12 sts remain.
Work 4 rows.
Shape shoulder
To decrease 12 sts over next 5 rows:
Cast off 4 sts at beginning of next row. Work 1 row.
Repeat these 2 rows once more. Cast off remaining 4 sts.
Second side
With right side of work facing, slip 10 sts at centre front to a stitch holder and rejoin yarn at right of remaining sts. Complete to match first side reversing shaping, beginning the shoulder shaping 1 row later, on a wrong-side row.

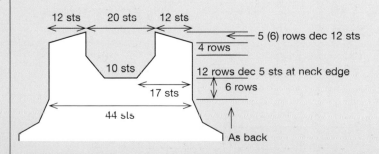

Shaping the waist

If you want your garment to be shaped at the waist, there are three main methods to consider:

Method 1: With a rib

Here, the waist area is pulled in by working a panel of firm rib. This rib panel usually needs to be quite deep (at least 7.5cm [3in]) or it will not be strong enough to control the fullness above it. This method works best in an elastic yarn such as wool that will return to shape after stretching. K2, P2 rib is more elastic than K1, P1 rib.

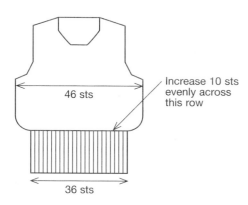

Increase 10 sts evenly across this row

46 sts

36 sts

As well as your main tension sample, you need another sample for the rib, made on smaller needles. Measure the main tension as usual, and measure the rib tension with the sample stretched (as much as you want it to be stretched when worn).
Calculate the number of stitches for the bust measurement of the main part in the usual way, using the main tension. (46 stitches on diagram).
Calculate the number of stitches for the waist measurement using the stretched rib tension. (36 sts on diagram.)
In our example, 10 sts will be increased evenly across the first row above the rib.
When working the bar increase (Kfb, page 132), 1 stitch becomes 2 stitches. To determine the spacing of the increases, subtract the number of increases from the rib stitches:
36 – 10 = 26. These 26 stitches must be divided into 11 groups, that is, one more group than the number of increases:
26 divided by 11 = 2, plus 4 extra.
Therefore 2 stitches will be worked between the increases. At the beginning and end of the row, work half the extra stitches, plus a group of 2: 2 + 2 = 4 sts. After working the rib, the instructions will read:
Change to larger needles.
Increase row: K4, [Kfb, K2] 9 times, Kfb, K4. 46 sts.
Continue in stocking stitch.

You may find after measuring both your tension samples that you need more stitches for the rib than for the main part – if so, you will need to calculate a decreasing row with evenly spaced decreases in a similar way to above.

Method 2: At the side seams

In this example the side edges are shaped into the waist, and then out again to the underarm. Only gentle shaping is recommended, otherwise the side seams will not lie smoothly, so the waist will not be clearly defined. This method works well with a garment of hip length or longer.

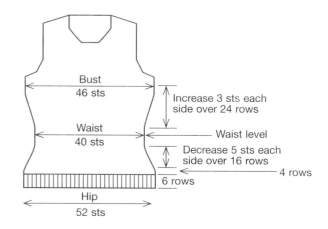

Bust
46 sts

Increase 3 sts each side over 24 rows

Waist
40 sts

Waist level

Decrease 5 sts each side over 16 rows

4 rows

6 rows

Hip
52 sts

By fitting a toile, determine the widths required at the bust, waist and hip. At the side edge, mark the waist level, the beginning of the waist decreasing just above the hip bone and the beginning of the increasing 2.5cm (1 inch) or so above the waist. Alter your paper pattern accordingly.
Use the triangle method (see page 38) to calculate the decreasing and increasing at the side edges.
In our example, after working 6 rib rows and 4 stocking stitch rows, the waist decreasing begins:
Decrease 5 sts at each side over 16 rows. 40 sts remain.
Work 8 rows.
Then the increasing begins:
Increase 3 sts at each side over 24 rows. 46 sts.
(Followed by the armhole shaping.)

Method 3: With darts

Another way to shape a waist is by working darts (see page 133). Instead of working the decreases and increases at the side edges, these shapings are grouped together in two (or more) vertical lines, positioned where required. The shaping can be more closely fitted to the body than Method 2, and the silhouette will remain smooth. However in the case of a sweater with no fastenings, bear in mind that the garment will need to stretch when you put it on or take it off.

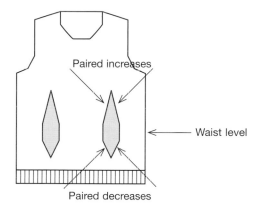

Here, two darts are placed on the front of a sweater, each one-quarter of the width in from a side edge.

Think of a dart as a section missing from the knitting (although there is no actual hole, because the knitting continues across the dart). Use the triangle method (see page 38) to calculate the shaping at each side of the 'missing' section. Darts are normally worked with paired decreases and increases to form a decorative detail. See page 133 for the method of working a dart.

This sweater has been knitted in a medium-weight wool mix, note the use of moss stitch to add detail at the neckline, cuff and hem. The garment is slim fitting, with waist shaping, which when combined with the bow on the neckline creates a very feminine garment.

USING STITCHES

Once you have grasped the basic principles of repeat, you can develop and alter stitches to create your own variations. Stitches can also be used to draw attention to particular areas on the garment, such as shaping. When you are designing your garments, keep in mind the small details. Consideration at the design stage will ensure that your garment has a professional finish.

New stitch
tension swatches

Before introducing decorative stitches to your garment designs, you must first create a tension swatch using those stitches.

As you become more confident with your pattern-writing skills, you may want to develop your design ideas using a variety of knitting stitches. The same principles apply to creating a tension swatch whether you use a plain or highly decorative stitch.

You will need
- Yarn
- The right-sized knitting needles for your yarn
- Tape measure
- Paper and pencil
- Sharp scissors

Tension samples for all the stitches you use

If rib is being used as a cuff or hem with the remaining rows on the garment in another stitch, you should sample both the rib and the main stitches to compare the relative tension. You may be able to use the same number of stitches for both areas, relying on the elasticity of the rib to shape the garment. Or you may need to cast on fewer stitches for the rib, and increase several stitches evenly across the first main row, to obtain the fit you require. Calculating a multiple increase row is described on page 96.

How to knit a patterned tension swatch

Following the principles discussed on pages 20–21, you can knit a patterned swatch. You need to ensure that you cast on enough stitches and knit enough rows to show the repeat. This swatch on the right is knitted using waffle stitch (see below) on UK 6mm, US size 10 needles with chunky yarn.

The waffle stitch pattern repeats over units of 2 stitches, so you need to cast on a multiple of this number. This example is worked over 20 stitches. The pattern repeats over 4 rows, so you need to work this number of rows several times to see the full effect.
The patterned tension swatch is 20 stitches wide, and 20 rows high.
The measurements are:
20 stitches = 14cm or 5.5in.
20 rows = 12.5cm or 5in.
Work the calculation for stitches and rows in the same way as for a plain swatch:
20 stitches divided by 14cm (5.5in) = 1.43 stitches to 1cm or 3.64 stitches to 1in.
20 rows divided by 12.5cm (5in) = 1.6 rows to 1cm or 4 rows to 1in.

Waffle stitch

Description: A heavy, three-dimensional stitch; worked in DK, it is suitable for a jacket, coat or blanket.
Multiple of 2 sts.
K1 blw: Knit one below: Insert right needle front to back in centre of the loop just below next stitch. Make a knit stitch, dropping the stitch from the left needle in the usual way, at the same time pulling upwards to elongate the stitch. Always work a normal stitch between two K1 blw.

Rows 1 and 2: Knit.
Row 3: *K1, K1 blw*, repeat * to * to end.
Row 4: *pick up the long (top) thread produced by the K1 blw and K it together with the st on the needle, K1*, repeat * to * to end.
Row 5: *K1 blw, K1*, repeat * to * to end.
Row 6: *K1, K the next st tog with the long thread as for row 4*, repeat * to * to end.
Rep Rows 3 to 6.

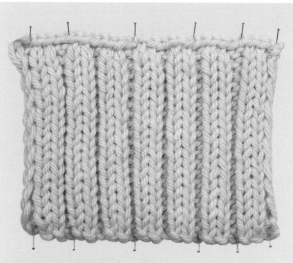

How to measure a rib swatch

Follow the same principles as above to knit a rib swatch. The rib can either be measured at a stretch or in a relaxed state. If the garment will be worn with the rib stretched, measure the tension with the rib stretched by the desired amount. You will notice that when your rib is stretched the depth of the rows decreases. Pin the swatch at the desired amount of stretch and measure the tension in the usual way.

SEE ALSO
Making and measuring a tension swatch
For more information on making and measuring a tension swatch, turn to pages 20–21.

Essential techniques
Essential knitting know-how is detailed on pages 128–135.

Shaping the waist with a rib
How to calculate multiple increases across a row is detailed on page 96.

All-over textures

Design your knitwear with all-over stitch patterns.

Try experimenting with textured patterns such as rib, crunchy, lace and other textures. Use them all over or on areas of your design.

Rib patterns

Rib stitch patterns are often used at the edges of garments because they tend to lie flat without rolling. Depending on the yarn used, they may be elastic and therefore return to size after stretching, suitable for body-conscious designs. Worked more loosely, rib patterns usually drape well, with an elegant vertical emphasis.

Stitch multiples

Repeating stitch patterns require a certain number of stitches, for example:
'Even number of stitches' means any number that divides by 2, or
'Multiple of 6 stitches plus 5' means any number of groups of 6 stitches (such as 7 x 6 = 42 sts), plus 5 more (42 + 5 = 47 sts).
Where a garment piece requires shaping, practise increasing and/or decreasing on a patterned swatch, to figure out how to keep the pattern constant as you work the shaping.

Knotted rib

There are many variations on the basic rib stitch patterns. This knotted rib, for example, will behave in the same way as a basic rib, but the arrangement of little knots adds extra texture.

Requires a multiple of 6 sts, plus 5.
Special abbreviation: MK = make knot: K into front, back and front of next st (making 3 sts on right needle), pass 1st and 2nd of these sts over 3rd st, leaving 1 st on right needle.
Row 1: P2, * K1 tbl, P2, * repeat from * to * to end.
Row 2: K2, * P1 tbl, K2, * repeat from * to * to end.
Row 3: P2, * MK, P2, K1 tbl, P2, * repeat from * to * to last 3 sts, MK, P2.
Row 4: as row 2
Rows 5 and 6: as rows 1 and 2
Row 7: P2, * K1 tbl, P2, MK, P2, * repeat from * to * to last 3 sts, K1 tbl, P2.
Row 8: as row 2.
Repeat these 8 rows.

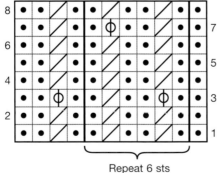

Repeat 6 sts

KEY   • P on rs row, K on ws row   ╱ K1 tbl on rs row P1 tbl on ws row   φ MK (make knot) as special abbreviation   ☐ K on rs row, P on ws row   ◿ K2tog on WS row   ∪ inc1 as special abbreviation

Crunchy textures

There's a huge choice of textured stitch patterns. You can use them as all-over patterns, or combine them with smoother stitches to highlight a particular area of a design. Below are just two examples for you to try.

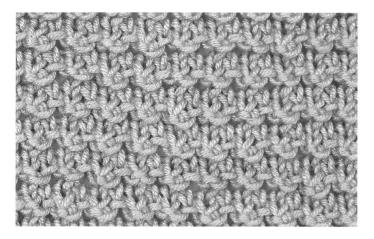

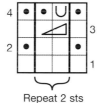

Repeat 2 sts

Pebble stitch

This textured stitch repeats over only four rows, making it easy to incorporate into shaped garment pieces. It forms a knobbly texture with a horizontal arrangement.

Requires an even number of sts, plus 2 selvedge sts (see page 134).
Special abbreviation: incl = make one: lift the horizontal thread lying between the needle tips and knit it (this increases 1 st, leaving a small hole).
Row 1: K.
Row 2: K1, P to last st, K1.
Row 3: K1, * K2tog, * repeat from * to * to last st, K1.
Row 4: K1, * K1, incl, * repeat from * to * to last st, K1.
Repeat these 4 rows.
(Do not check the stitch count after Row 3.)

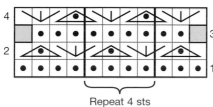

Repeat 4 sts

Popcorn stitch

Popcorn or Trinity stitch is formed by making a double increase in one stitch followed by a double decrease in the next. It is a popular choice for a panel in an Aran sweater. Note that at the end of Row 2, there are 2 stitches fewer than you started with. At the end of Row 4, the pattern comes back to the starting number.

Requires a multiple of 4 sts, plus 3.
Special abbreviation: KPK = (knit 1, purl 1, knit 1) all into the next st.
Row 1 (RS row): P.
Row 2: * P3 tog, KPK, *, repeat from * to * to last 3 sts, P3 tog.
Row 3: P.
Row 4: * KPK, P3 tog *, repeat from * to * to last st, KPK.

P3tog   KPK as special abbreviation   no stitch

Lace patterns

A hole in a lace pattern is usually made by increasing a stitch, either with a yarn over (yo, page 132) or with a small hole increase (incl, as for Pebble stitch, page 101). For every increase, there will be a corresponding decrease, usually (but not always) on the same row. The arrangement of the increases and decreases, and the methods used to work them, determine the lace pattern. Below are just two examples, but there are hundreds to choose from.

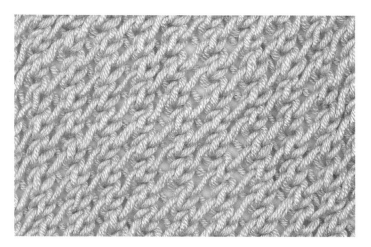

Lace mesh

This stitch forms a loose, flexible fabric with a diagonal emphasis. The fabric is also reversible: front and back are identical in appearance.

Requires an even number of sts, plus 2 selvedge sts (see page 134).
Row 1: K1, * yo, K2tog, * repeat from * to * to last st, K1.
Repeat this row.

Repeat 2 sts

Feather and fan

In this traditional Shetland lace stitch, groups of increases (yarn overs) alternate with balancing groups of decreases, causing the knitted rows to move up and down, forming wavy top and bottom edges, which require no further edging. The wave formation is emphasized by knitting every 4th row to form a ridge.

Requires a multiple of 12 sts, plus 1.
Note: to form a firm lower edge as shown, K 1 row before commencing pattern.
Row 1: K.
Row 2: P.
Row 3: K1, * (K2tog) twice, (yo, K1) three times, yo, (skpo) twice, K1, * repeat from * to * to end.
Row 4: K.
Repeat these 4 rows.

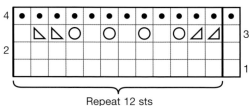

Repeat 12 sts

KEY ● P on rs row, K on ws row ☐ K on rs row, P on ws row ◺ skpo ◯ yo ◿ K2tog on rs row, skpo on ws row ⚬ MC as special abbreviation

Experimenting with stitch

Once you have become familiar with how a particular stitch pattern is formed, you can try changing the formation slightly to create your own variations – charts like those shown here can be drawn on squared paper for reference. For example:

Knotted rib could be worked with more purl stitches between the ribs, or with the knots in a different arrangement.

Pebble stitch could be varied by working more stocking stitch rows between the patterned rows, or by repeating rows 3 and 4 several times.

Lace patterns can be varied by working inc 1 instead of yo, or vice versa, or by working ws rows as K instead of P.

Other stitch patterns such as Popcorn stitch or Feather and fan can be adapted by introducing coloured stripes.

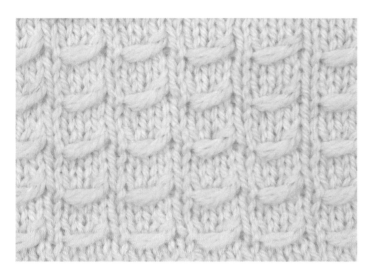

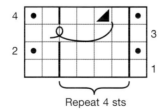

Repeat 4 sts

Comma stitch

This Comma stitch uses an unusual stitch formation to make the 'commas', arranged in straight rows. This stitch would also lend itself to experimentation: try spacing the 'commas' further apart, or work them on every right side row to make columns of 'commas'.

Requires a multiple of 4 sts plus 1, plus 2 selvedge sts (see page 134).

Special abbreviation: MC = make comma: K3, slip these 3 sts back onto left needle without twisting them, insert right needle to left of these 3 sts and draw through a long loop onto right needle, then slip same 3 sts back again from left needle to right needle.

Row 1: K.
Row 2: K1, P to last st, K1.
Row 3: K1, * K1, MC, * repeat from * to * to last 2 sts, K2.
Row 4: K1, * P3, P next st tog with comma loop, * repeat from * to * to last 2 sts, P1, K1.
Repeat these 4 rows.

SEE ALSO
Making and measuring a tension swatch
For more information on making and measuring a tension swatch, turn to pages 20–21.

Essential techniques
Essential knitting know-how is detailed on pages 128–135.

◤ P next st tog with comma loop

Shaping with stitches

Ways to use stitches to highlight shaping.

When it comes to shaping, stitches alone can be used to great effect. In this section you will be shown examples of stitches combined with shaping to inspire your designs. An easy-to-understand chart explains exactly how the stitch has been combined with shaping.

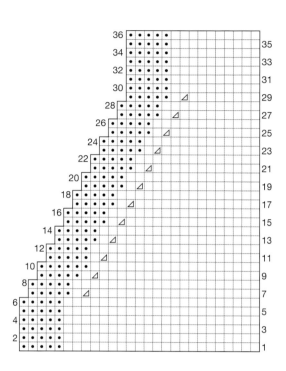

Emphasize shaping with purl stitch

In this example the band of purl stitches running along the edge of the knitted sample highlights the shaping. It has been worked by decreasing 12 stitches over 23 rows. Each decrease (K2tog on RS row) is followed by K1, P5 at the left edge of the sample.

Moving rib with single moss stitch

In this example the rib has been angled across the swatch by moving all of the rib stitches to the right of the work. The rib stitches disappear off to the right-hand side of the sample and single moss stitch is introduced on the left-hand side. The cast-on edge has 30 stitches of two-by-two rib. At the bound-off edge there are 18 stitches of single moss stitch and 12 stitches of rib.

The rib is angled by decreasing at the right edge and increasing at the left edge of the rib.

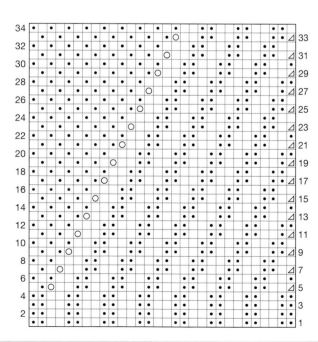

KEY   ● P on rs row, k on ws row   ☐ K on rs row, P on ws row   ○ yo   ◿ K2 tog   ◺ skpo

Moving rib

In this sample, the rib has been moved to follow the contours of the body. You will need to make a tension swatch of rib and work out the shaping following the method shown on page 99.

The two central ribs move outwards by one stitch on every other row, creating a widening central panel in reverse stocking stitch. To plot the rib movement, draw on your paper pattern. Plot the rib on graph paper to work out the stitches to be moved on each row.

Cable

Cable panels can be used to shape a garment. Make a cable swatch and a main stitch swatch, and compare the widths: The cable swatch will be narrower. Carefully positioned cables will draw in the knitted fabric for an elegant shape without increasing or decreasing.

SEE ALSO
Essential techniques
Essential knitting know-how is detailed on pages 128–135.

Matching patterns

When using patterns it is important to match them at the joining points, such as the sides, armholes and shoulder seams. This can be done by plotting the pattern onto your paper pattern, and matching the pieces together. Alternatively, you may prefer to count the number of rows from the shoulder point to the armhole and the sleeve cap to the armhole, and plot the repeat of the pattern into the rows. In this example the stripes have been matched and seamed together down the centre. There may be some amount of difference due to shaping, but it is best to match patterns when possible.

Part 4:

Embellishments

A great way to personalize or add small designer details to your garments is to use embellishment. This section features Swiss darning, appliqué and embroidery techniques and the use of trims, illustrated with specifically designed samples.

Embroidery

Embroidered embellishments can add interest
and texture to your knitted garments.

Embroidery can be used as an all-over design to enhance a
knitted stitch, or a single motif can draw attention to one area of
a garment, and can work well with other types of embellishment
such as beads or sequins. Necklines and cuffs, in particular, can
be highlighted and enhanced by the use of embroidery.

   The demonstrations featured here will introduce you to
some of the basic stitches that you may want to use on
your own designs.

You will need

- Knitted garment or sample
- Embroidery hoop (optional)
- Blunt yarn needle
- Yarn, thread or ribbon
- Sharp scissors

*Embroidery and appliqué
techniques (see page
112) were combined to
create the striking horse
design on the front of
this sweater.*

Swiss darning

Swiss darning (also known as duplicate stitch) exactly copies the
structure of a knitted stitch. It is best used for outline designs
because large areas of duplicate stitch can thicken the knitted
fabric, making it less flexible.

   Once mastered, Swiss darning can be used to great effect,
and can replace intarsia or Fair Isle. It can be a very dramatic
technique when used with different weights or textured yarns.

1 Bring the needle out at the base of the
knitted stitch to be duplicated. Pass the
needle behind the two 'legs' of the stitch
above. Pull through.

2 Insert the needle again at the base
of the same knitted stitch where it first
emerged, and bring it out at the base of
the next knitted stitch to be duplicated.
Here, a line of Swiss darning is being
worked from right to left. Repeat as
required, counting the stitches carefully.

Tension issues

The effect will be more realistic if the
stitches match the tension of the knitting.
Some knitters find it helpful to place the
knitting in an embroidery hoop to keep it
flat and ensure that the stitches do not
pull too tight.

Freestyle Swiss darning

Swiss darning can be done with a mix of yarns on a fine knitted base. The embroidery can be used in a very free way, with the stitches being carried up and to the side.

Note the unusual placement of the embroidery, adding interest to the back of the garment.

Using a graphed image

Here duplicate stitch has been used to create an image within the knitted stitch. This is best achieved by charting the designed image onto graph paper. In this example each stitch is represented by one square on the graph paper.

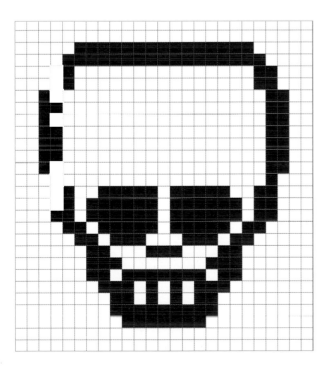

Freestyle embroidery

Freestyle embroidery may be worked across a plain knitted background; the examples below are shown on stocking stitch knitting. Follow the embroidery guidelines opposite.

Backstitch Use this stitch for outlines and fine lines. Bring the needle through from the back of the work. From the front and in one motion, take the needle through to the back a short distance along to the right, then draw back through the work to the front the same distance along to the left from the beginning of the stitch. Continue from right to left by inserting the needle through from front to back at the point where the last stitch emerged.

Chain stitch Chain stitch can be used in a continuous line to mark out shapes or fill in areas, and can work well as a detail running along a neckline or cuff. Chain stitch also mimics the elasticity of the background knitting.

Bring the needle through from the back. * In one motion, take the yarn through from front to back at the point where the first yarn came through to the front to create a loop. Bring the needle back through to the front a short distance along to the left and through the centre of the loop. Tighten and repeat from *.

At the end of the line, hold down the last chain loop with a small stitch over the loop, as shown for lazy daisy stitch, below.

French knots This stitch is often used within a floral pattern, but French knots can also be used as small spots, or as a fill to add texture. This stitch works well with thicker yarns, but do experiment with materials, since this technique can also be worked in ribbon.

Bring the needle through where required and wrap the yarn twice around the needle. Holding the yarn taut, insert the needle one knitted strand away from where it emerged. (Don't insert the needle in exactly the same place, or the knot will disappear through to the back of the knitting.) Pull through gently.

Taking embroidery further

There are many publications that explain fully and in depth how to use embroidery stitches. Hunt out books in charity shops for vintage design ideas.

Stem stitch This stitch makes a flowing continuous line, so can be used to edge a motif or link flowers together. Bring the needle through from the back of the work, then insert from front to back a short distance to the right at a slight angle and out again, about halfway along the stitch. Each stitch overlaps the previous one by about half its length.

Lazy daisy stitch Single chain stitches may be arranged to form little flowers. Hold down the loop of each chain with a small stitch. Make a chain stitch as described above, but instead of making a running sequence of stitches, sew a small stitch over the top of the chain to hold the loop in place. Repeat this in the formation of a small flower, each chain representing one petal.

Embroidery guidelines

- Use a blunt yarn needle to avoid splitting the stitches.
- Don't pull your stitches too tight, since embroidery can distort the knitting. If you find it difficult to control your stitches, use an embroidery hoop, but be careful not to overstretch the knitting when using the hoop.
- Do not carry the embroidery yarn across the back of the garment, since long 'floats' can get caught and pull.
- When working the embroidery, use short to medium lengths of thread or yarn, no longer than 50cm (20in) to avoid tangles.
- Secure all ends of yarn on the back of the knitting by running the needle through the back of the embroidered stitches.
- Ensure that the eye of your needle is large enough to accommodate the yarn, but not too big to pass through the knitting.
- Yarns of different thicknesses work well in embroidery and can add interest.

Blanket stitch Often used on felted garments, blanket stitch works well as an edging, and can be combined effectively with appliqué. Use unusual yarns or threads to add interest.

Working from left to right, bring the needle through the piece from the back, approximately one row in from the edge of the fabric. From the front, thread the needle through to the back, one stitch to the right, with the tip inside the loop of yarn, and pull through.

Whip stitch Work a line of a running stitch (simply in and out of the knitting), then pick an unusual yarn, ribbon or thread to weave in and out to create interest. This stitch works well as an edging on a neckline or opening.

The embroidered design on this sweater makes use of a variety of different stitches. Clockwise from the top: grey stem stitch star outline; red French knot star; whip stitch star outline; yellow and blue chain stitch star.

Appliqué

A detailed look at this versatile
embellishment technique.

Appliqué is normally used to translate images onto
sewn items, with shaped pieces applied to a base to
create an image or pattern. However, the technique
can also be adapted for use on knitted fabrics.

When using woven and knitted fabrics together, ideally pick a
fabric that is of a similar weight to the knitted one. If your fabric
is too heavy, it will distort the shape of your knitted garment.

The difference in structure between the fabrics will mean that
the knitted areas will stretch, whereas the woven ones will not,
so take care when using appliqué around a neckline because
it may limit the ability of the garment to stretch over the head.

You will need

- Knitted garment or sample
- Fabric of similar weight to
  knitted sample
- Sharp scissors
- Iron and ironing board
- Iron-on interfacing
- Iron-on fusible webbing or
  fabric glue
- Sewing needle and thread

Using webbing and interfacing

Iron-on interfacing (see below) can be used to stabilize the fabric
before cutting out the shapes. Iron it onto the back of the fabric
and mark out the shape before cutting.

If you want to attach the shapes to the knitting before sewing,
use iron-on fusible webbing or fabric glue and place the shapes
in the desired arrangements. Bond as instructed with the
product and allow to dry or cool before starting sewing.

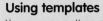

*Knit-on-knit appliqué was used
to create the flower design on
this swatch.*

Using templates

You can use pattern-paper templates to create
your appliqué shapes. Use the helpful grid
marks on pattern paper to draw up your
shapes, mark out the shapes on your fabric
and then cut out. If you want to turn in the
edges of your shape, cut 6mm (¼in) outside
the marked outline.

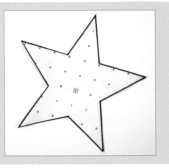

Appliqué fabric onto knitted fabric

Interesting effects can be achieved by using appliqué to combine fabric and knitting in one garment.

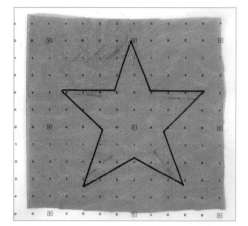

1 Cut out the desired shape from the woven fabric, in this case a transparent red fabric, that is to be applied, using iron-on interfacing if preferred. Iron the edges to the wrong side (unless you are using fusible webbing or interfacing).

2 Before stitching, you may want to attach the fabric shapes in position on the knitting with iron-on fusible webbing or fabric glue. The pieces are normally sewn in place with either straight stitch or satin stitch. You may choose to embellish the edges with knitted trims, tape or a different stitch.

3 In this example, the appliqué star has been attached with blanket stitch.

Appliqué knit-on-knit

This technique avoids all the problems associated with combining knit and woven fabrics.

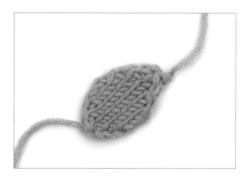

1 Knit the desired shape: In this case, a simple leaf shape.

2 Attach the knitted shapes to the knitted fabric using matching yarn and tiny stitches.

Developing the technique

For more information on appliqué, look for specialist books in libraries, craft shops or charity shops.

Design details

Interest can be added by layering shapes and combining appliqué with other knit techniques, such as embroidery or stitch details. Shapes can be left to hang free or combined with other decorations such as pom-poms or tassels (see page 116). This example combines embroidery with a knitted appliqué leaf to create a cherry design. The appliqué leaf was stitched only at the points to give it a three-dimensional quality

Trims and fastenings

How to use trims and fastenings to add interest and shape to a knitted garment.

Trims and fastenings are often one of the last things to be considered when designing a garment, but they can be used to give a garment identity and add a designer finish. The following illustrations depict a number of options for trims and fastenings that may be used to inspire your own designs.

Trims

Rib Besides its practical uses, rib can also be used as a design feature, placed at the waist, extended at the cuff or combined with a stripe to add a sporty feel.

Stripes Stripes can be used either horizontally or vertically to add interest to an edge. Knit a length of striped tape – four or five stitches wide – and sew to the garment.

When a whole garment is striped, the stripes can be either matched or deliberately mismatched. In this example, a chequerboard effect has been created.

Purl-stitch roll A small roll makes a subtle yet effective trim, which can be knitted integrally into the design if planned in advance. In this example, a contrasting colour has been used. The roll is worked in stocking stitch, which naturally rolls with the purl side out. Take care to cast off loosely.

Drawstring
Often used as an alternative to a rib, this drawstring is threaded through a row of holes. Details can be added by picking an unusual cord and adding finishing touches such as pom-poms or tassels. Alternatively, you could knit your own cord and add interest by using stripes or a textured stitch.

Fastenings

Buttons Search for buttons that are appropriate for your design, perhaps by visiting vintage shops, markets or online shops to source interesting and unusual examples. You can also buy kits that allow you to cover buttons to match your knitted garments exactly.

Add interest to a cuff by using more than the required number of buttons.

Hooks and eyes An interesting alternative to buttons, hooks and eyes now come in a variety of sizes and finishes, from metal to plastic, and can be used with knitted tapes to fasten a garment.

Ties Knit your own ties to fasten your garment. While ties are often used on wrap-around garments, they can also be very effective when used at the neck and cuffs. Design details can be added by scaling the ties up or down, or using contrasting colours or textures of yarn or stitches.

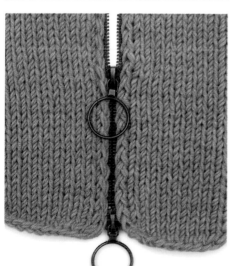

Zips Zips can be difficult to use in knitted garments; however, if care is taken when assembling the garment, they can be very effective. If needed, use a woven tape to help stabilize the knitted fabric when sewing the zip in.

SEE ALSO
Essential techniques
Essential knitting know-how is detailed on pages 128–135.

This sweater has drawstrings at the sleeves and a frilled neckline (see page 73).

Pom-poms, tassels and fringes

Add a fun touch to your project.

A pom-pom or tassel on cord ties to fasten a sweater, on gathered sleeve cuffs or on a belt tie can add an interesting detail to your knitwear. Fringing is commonly seen on scarves but could be added to garments too. For example, add a fringe to a collar or to the opening or hem of a cardigan.

Add pom-poms to hats and scarves, or use them to trim the ends of tie fastenings on a jacket or cardigan.

Pom-poms, tassels and fringes are yarn hungry, and if the notion of adding such a trim is at the back of your mind from the start, buy extra yarn. How much extra will depend on the thickness and length of the fringe or tassel, or the density, size and number of the pom-poms. As soon as you can, make a sample trim, noting how it was made and its weight. Multiply the weight of the trim by its frequency to calculate how much yarn you will need.

Making a pom-pom

There are many brands of pom-pom makers on the market, but the easiest method is to use two doughnut-shaped circles of card. Start by determining the size of the pom-pom, then, if you are using DK-weight yarn, draw two outer circles about 10 per cent larger than the diameter desired. (This extra 10 per cent is for tidying and trimming the ball into shape at the end.)

If you are using a lighter-weight yarn, reduce this margin; if you are using a heavier-weight yarn, increase it. Draw two smaller circles inside the first two circles. (The larger these holes are, the denser the pom-pom; the smaller the holes, the looser the pom-pom and the more likely it is to be slightly oval.) A good, medium-sized pom-pom is achieved with a second circle half the diameter of the finished pom-pom size.

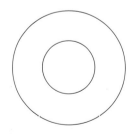

To make a pom-pom: Cut two doughnut shapes from card in the size required.

1 Cut out the doughnut shapes from the card and, holding them together, wind the yarn around the card, working from inside the hole, around the card and back through the hole, each new wrap lying next to the last. Continue until the centre hole is filled, threading a needle with the yarn for the last wraps.

2 Using a pair of sharp scissors and cutting a few strands at a time, cut around the pom-pom edge between the two discs. Pry the discs slightly apart and tie a length of yarn tightly around the centre of the pom-pom. Remove the discs – it may be necessary to cut them. Tousle the yarn strands and trim the pom-pom to make a neat ball.

Making a tassel

Start by cutting a piece of card the depth of the desired tassel. It does not have to be very wide and need not be very thick – just solid enough not to buckle as the yarn is wrapped around it.

1 Hold the end of a length of yarn with your thumb halfway up the length of card and wrap the yarn around the card by moving down to the bottom of the card, around the top, over the top and back again. Continue until you reach the desired tassel thickness, and stop at the bottom of the card, leaving 2.5cm (1in) free. Note the number of wraps.

2 Thread a second length of yarn through a needle. Pass this under the wrapped yarn and tie it around the tassel at the top edge of the card. Cut the tassel along the bottom edge and remove the yarn. The start and end of the wrapped yarn will hang slightly lower. Trim the 'skirt'.

3 Pass the second length of yarn threaded through a needle down through the tassel to the base of the desired tassel head. Wrap the yarn around the tassel once and pass the needle behind and over the start of the wrap. Wrapping in the opposite direction, wrap the tassel as many times as desired and secure the end by bringing the needle out at the top.

Tassel variations

Padded tassel
Wadding is inserted in the centre of the top of the skirt, below the securing knot, before the tassel head is finished. This wadding provides a secure base for embellishment as well as altering the tassel head shape.

Pom-pom tassel
Sometimes the head of a tassel can seem rather flat. For this tassel, the skirt at the end of Step 2 (above) was used to secure a pom-pom.

Making a fringe

Experiment with fluffy or bulky yarns, many or single yarns, and the spacing along the edge you are fringing to create different effects. Note that too many fringes attached along an edge can cause the edge to splay and ripple slightly. This distance will vary from fabric to fabric, and from fringe yarn to fringe yarn.

Start by cutting a piece of card the depth of the desired fringe. Wrap the yarn around the card, then cut the yarn along one edge to create yarn lengths double the depth of the fringe.

Using a crochet hook, insert the hook through a stitch or space between two stitches on the edge to be fringed, either from front to back or back to front. Fold a length of cut yarn in half and loop the fold over the crochet hook. Draw the crochet hook and the loop of yarn through the edge, place the yarn ends over the hook, and draw them through the first loop to knot in place. Continue to work along the edge. For an even fringe, work throughout, either front to back or back to front and with equal spacing.

Adding beads
and sequins to knitting

Use beads and sequins to add colour
and texture to knitwear.

Although you can work different
colours and textures into your
knitting with yarn and stitch,
it can be fun to use other
embellishments, such as beads.
Be sure to choose the right beads
for your project, thread them onto
the knitting yarn as described
below, then use the method
given to knit beads in as your
work proceeds.

Choosing beads or sequins

Washability Depending on your
project, you may need washable
beads or sequins.

Weight The knitted yarn needs to be
strong enough to support the beads
comfortably, without sagging, so if you
are working with a soft yarn avoid beads
that are large and heavy. Beads may be
made of plastic, glass, wood, metal or
ceramic. Plastic and wooden beads are
generally lightweight, whereas glass,
metal and ceramic beads may be
heavier and add considerably to the
weight of your project.

Hole size Beads to be knitted in should
have holes that are large enough to let
the bead move easily along the yarn.
If you want to use small beads, you'll
need to sew them in place. Beads or
sequins to be sewn on may have holes
of any size.

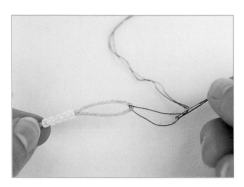

1 Work to where the bead is required. Slide
the bead up the yarn. Bring the yarn forwards
between the needles with the bead to the
front and slip the next stitch purlwise.

Threading beads onto yarn

If it is not possible to thread the knitting
yarn directly through the bead, use this
method: Thread a fine needle using both
ends of a piece of sewing thread. Place
the yarn through the loop of thread, then
pass the beads over the eye of the
needle, along the sewing thread and
onto the yarn. Thread on all the beads
you need before you start knitting.

Knitting in beads with a slip stitch

Placing beads with a slip stitch is done
using garter stitch or stocking stitch on
the right side of the work. Beads can be
placed every other stitch and every other
row. The bead falls directly in front of the
slipped stitch.

2 Keep the bead as close to the knitting as
possible, holding it in front of the slipped
stitch with a finger or thumb if necessary,
then take the yarn back between the
needles, leaving the bead in front. Knit the
next stitch firmly.

Sewing on beads or sequins

To sew on beads or sequins, use a beading needle (a very slim sewing needle with a small eye), or any sharp sewing needle that fits easily through the beads or sequins.

Sewing on beads

Use thread double and secure it firmly with tiny backstitches behind the bead. Bring the needle through to the right side of the work and thread a bead onto the needle. Take a small stitch through the knitting and pull the thread through. Pass the needle through the bead again, then take the needle through to the wrong side of the work. Make another small backstitch on the wrong side, where it will be hidden by the bead.

Attaching a sequin with a bead

A neat way to attach sequins is to secure each one with a tiny bead at the centre. Secure the thread, bring the needle up where required, thread on a sequin and then a small bead. Take the needle back down through the centre of the sequin. Repeat the stitch through the bead once more, then secure the thread on the wrong side.

The embellishment on this sweater was inspired by intarsia, a knitting method used to create patterns with different-coloured yarns. The pattern is made up from fur discs.

A traditional cricket sweater was used as inspiration for this piece, which has been embellished all over with sequins to highlight the cable pattern and the neckline.

Part 5:
Basic knitting know-how

This section introduces the basic knitting tools and discusses the qualities of the various yarns, types of knitting needles and the differences between them. Following this, you'll find a refresher course covering all the essential knitting skills and knowledge you'll need to use the techniques described in this book.

Choosing a yarn

A look at the variety of yarns available to the knitter.

There are many types of yarn, all with different qualities and attributes, and your choice of yarn will affect the whole garment. When choosing a yarn, start by asking yourself some sensible questions:

When and where will the garment be worn – daytime; to work; evening; occasional; outside?

What is the purpose of the garment – comfort; to keep warm; glamour; layering?

Is washing a consideration?

Is expense a consideration? Some yarns can be very expensive, while others are more economical.

You should also give thought to how long you want the project to take. A very fine yarn will have to be knitted on small needles and will need more stitches, whereas a chunky yarn can be knitted on thicker needles much more quickly.

Tip

When buying yarn, always keep one yarn ball band for reference. Pin it to the tension swatch and keep it safe, together with any leftover yarn and spare buttons. This gives you a handy reference for washing instructions and provides for emergency repairs or alterations.

Wool, lambswool and wool mixes

Wool is an adaptable yarn that can be used in a variety of garments. It is a natural, breathable fibre that will keep you warm in the winter; however, it needs to be washed carefully because it will shrink with heat. Some people are allergic to wool.

There has been a resurgence in the use of special-breed sheep to produce wool, and this wool can be an ethical choice for yarn companies producing eco-friendly yarns.

Lambswool is a softer variety of yarn, and will fluff up when hand-washed.

Blended yarns are common. Often wool is mixed with cotton or acrylic to avoid shrinkage when washing. Most winter-weight hand-knit yarns contain some wool. Details of the percentage can be found on the label.

Yarns shown here from top to bottom: Merino wool; worsted wool; cashmere and wool blend.

Cashmere

Traditionally the most luxurious and expensive of yarns, cashmere is very lightweight and soft. It is a breathable natural fibre and a good choice for luxury or classic garments. Cashmere garments will last a long time if looked after with care.

Yarn companies now produce blends of cashmere, often mixed with cotton or silk, to help reduce the cost.

Pure cashmere yarn.

Cotton

Often used for summer garments, pieces knitted with cotton will help keep the wearer cool. Cotton is a good choice for lightweight garments for layering.

Cotton yarns appear crisp and feel light, and interest can be added by using a cotton yarn with a twist or slub. Cotton is often mixed with linen.

Cotton garments should be dried flat when washed, since cotton becomes heavy when wet.

Cotton yarns (left): Aran-weight cotton and wool blend; cotton and synthetic blend.

Super-chunky yarns

Chunky yarns are perfect for the knitter who wants to create a garment quickly, and many chunky blended yarns are now very lightweight. Good for accessories, jackets and garments that will be worn outside.

Chunky yarns shown here from top to bottom, left to right: wool and silk blend; wool; unspun tops (wool); gently spun wool.

Fancy yarns

There is a variety of tapes and fancy yarns available, with blends including Lurex, mohair and rayon, that are good for evening or occasional wear. These yarns can add interest and texture to garments. However, be aware that such yarns often look very different when knitted up and can be difficult to use: not the best choice for the first-time knitter.

Fancy yarns shown here, clockwise from the top: Cotton twist with beads; viscose ribbon yarn; textured ribbon yarn; Lurex corded yarn; synthetic-mix mohair; feather yarn spun with man-made fibres and paper.

Materials and equipment

A guide to selecting the materials and equipment you'll need for your project.

All you need to create a knitted fabric are needles and yarn; however, there is a whole array of different needles available. Your choice of needle will be partly determined by your specific project, but also by personal preference. You will also need equipment for designing and adapting patterns, creating paper patterns and making toiles.

Stitch holders

Choosing needles

Knitting needles can also be known as knitting 'pins' or 'sticks', and are mainly sold in pairs. The most common type of knitting needle has a long, straight shaft that tapers at one end to allow the stitches to be formed, and has a stop on the other end to prevent the stitches from falling off. Other types of knitting needles include circular needles, double-pointed needles and cable needles.

Although you will find it easier, and in some cases cheaper, to buy your needles online, it is worth visiting a shop to try holding different types of needles. You will be using them for a generous period of time, so you want them to feel comfortable. Knitting needles not only come in different diameters to suit your choice of yarn, but also various lengths, so pick a pair that you can manoeuvre easily and that is long enough for the width of your project.

Needles are now produced from many different materials, so some of the most common types are illustrated here.

Stitch holders
These devices work like large safety pins, and are used for holding groups of stitches when working necklines (see page 74), for example.

Classic metal-coated needles
These needles are cheap and will last a lifetime. However, some knitters find them rather heavy.

Aluminium needles
These needles are very popular because they are lightweight and easy to use, durable and useful for swift knitting since the stitches slip easily.

Plastic needles
Lightweight, but susceptible to breaking, some plastic needles are reinforced to give extra strength. Large needles are often hollow to reduce weight.

Wooden needles
Most wooden needles now come from sustainable sources, such as bamboo. They are less likely to drop stitches due to the slightly rough finish of the wood, are lightweight and good for controlling slippery yarn.

Interchangeable needles
This system consists of a cord that is attached to two needle heads in the size that you require. Interchangeable needles are easy to use, and can be used for both circular and flat knitting.

Double-pointed needles
These are used mainly for circular knitting (socks, neckbands, etc) and are sold in sets of four or five.

Cable needles
Short, double-pointed needles that may be straight or kinked, used when working cable patterns.

Interchangeable needles

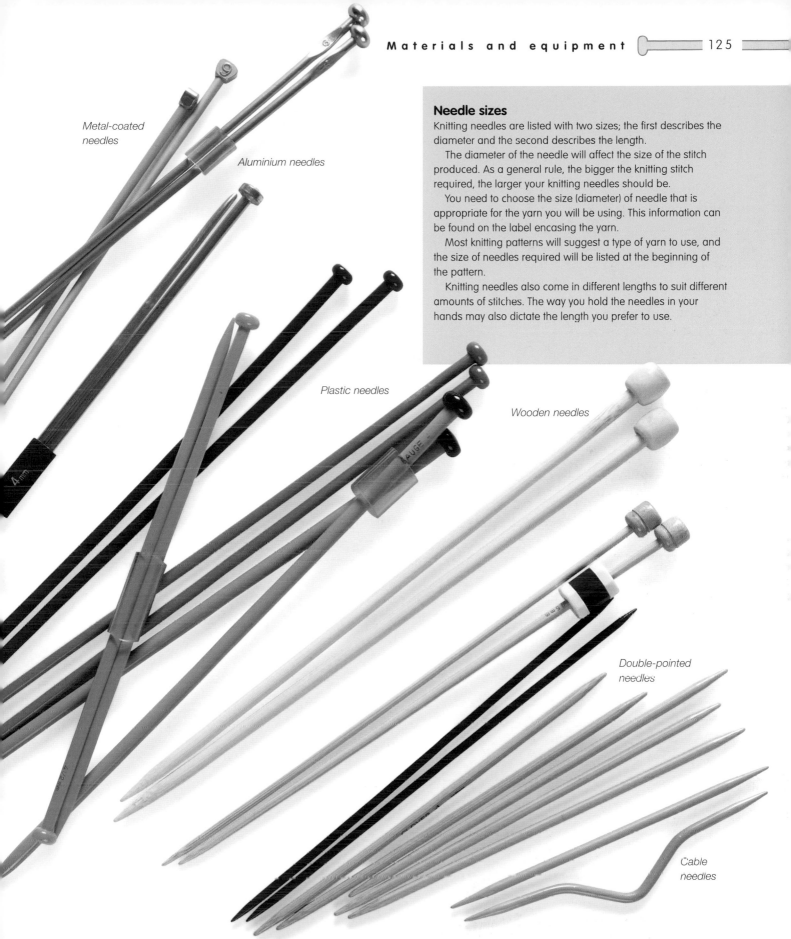

Metal-coated needles

Aluminium needles

Plastic needles

Wooden needles

Double-pointed needles

Cable needles

Needle sizes

Knitting needles are listed with two sizes; the first describes the diameter and the second describes the length.

The diameter of the needle will affect the size of the stitch produced. As a general rule, the bigger the knitting stitch required, the larger your knitting needles should be.

You need to choose the size (diameter) of needle that is appropriate for the yarn you will be using. This information can be found on the label encasing the yarn.

Most knitting patterns will suggest a type of yarn to use, and the size of needles required will be listed at the beginning of the pattern.

Knitting needles also come in different lengths to suit different amounts of stitches. The way you hold the needles in your hands may also dictate the length you prefer to use.

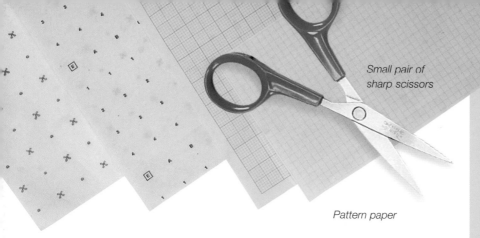

Small pair of
sharp scissors

Pattern paper

Other equipment

Spot-and-cross paper, marked paper, graph paper, alphabet paper

These large sheets of marked paper are used to draw up paper patterns. The guidelines on the paper can be used to check that vertical and horizontal lines are straight.

Dressmaking curves/French curves

These templates, made of plastic, wood or metal and available in a variety of shapes, act as guides when drawing curves on a paper pattern, for example to shape necklines.

Ruler

A ruler is used for measuring tension swatches and also can be useful for drawing out paper patterns (see page 36).

Tapestry needle

Blunt-tipped tapestry needles are essential for sewing seams and can also be used for embroidery (see page 108) and weaving in yarn ends.

Scissors

A small pair of pointed sharp scissors are used for cutting yarn. It's not advised to try to break yarn.

Notebook and pen

A notebook and pen are essential for noting down measurements, tension and converting measurements into stitches and rows.

Equipment and materials needed for making a toile

When designing your own knitting pattern it's important to check the fit of your garment before you start knitting. You can do this by making a toile (see page 42). The following items are essential for making and fitting a toile.

Jersey or other similar fabric

The fabric you use for making your toile should be of a similar weight to your chosen yarn in order to make an accurate representation of the finished garment. Use your tension swatch as reference when purchasing your fabric.

Dressmaking pins and safety pins

General-purpose pins are used to hold pieces of fabric together before sewing. They are suitable for medium-weight fabrics. Safety pins are good for securing the pieces of a toile you're trying on for fit.

Tailor's chalk

Tailor's chalk is a traditional material used for marking cloth and can be easily brushed away when finished. This is available in a variety of colours; use a colour that contrasts with your fabric.

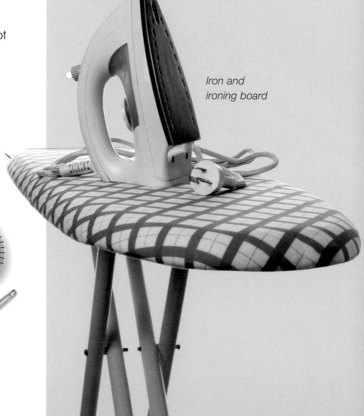

Iron and
ironing board

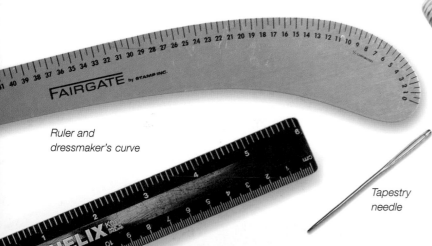

Ruler and
dressmaker's curve

Tapestry
needle

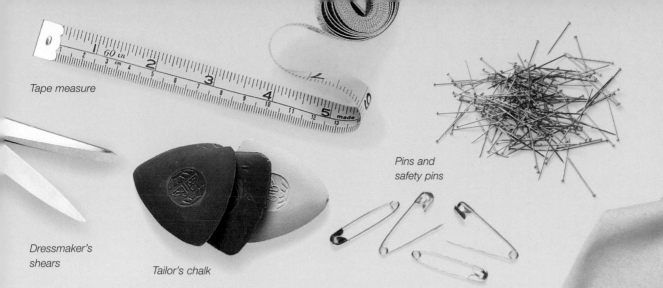

Tape measure

Dressmaker's shears

Tailor's chalk

Pins and safety pins

Sewing machine or needle and thread
A sewing machine is ideal for quickly sewing up the seams of your toiles; however, if you do not have a sewing machine, a needle and thread will work just as well.

Dressmaker's fabric shears
The long, straight, sharp blades of these shears give a smooth cut and are ideal for cutting fabric quickly. Often the handles are at an angle to the blades, so the blades can sit parallel to the cutting surface, ensuring the fabric remains flat. They should be used only on fabric.

Tape measure
A tape measure is essential for taking body measurements. Choose a good-quality tape measure that will neither unravel nor stretch. It should be at least 150 cm (60in) long, with measurements marked accurately from the very start of the tape.

Iron and ironing board
An iron and ironing board are essential for ironing fabrics, and are also useful for smoothing seams on your toiles. They are also essential when steaming or 'blocking' your knitted garment pieces (see page 58).

Dress forms
Dress forms can be used as an alternative to trying on a toile yourself. They allow you to try your toile out and to adjust garments for a better fit before final sewing. Adjustable dress forms are ideal models to start with. The dimensions can be easily adjusted to match your own or a friend's measurements.

Jersey fabric

Sewing machine

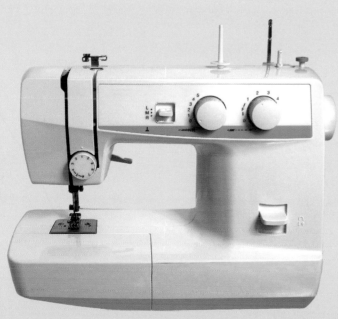

Dress form

Essential techniques

If you're a new knitter, you will find here all the information you need to get started and maybe even enough to attempt more ambitious stitches.

Ends

The end of yarn left after casting on should be a reasonable length so that it can be used for sewing up. The same applies to the end left after casting off. Ends left when a new colour is joined in should be darned in along a seam or row end on the wrong side and can also be very useful for covering up imperfections, such as awkward colour changes. Ends left while working a motif are better darned in behind the motif. Use a blunt-pointed tapestry needle for darning in.

Slipknot

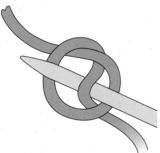 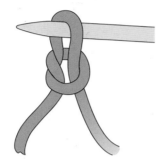

1 Putting a slipknot on the needle makes the first stitch of the cast-on. Loop the yarn around two fingers of the left hand, the ball end on top. Dip the needle into the loop, catch the ball end of the yarn and pull it through the loop.

2 Pull the ends of the yarn to tighten the knot. Tighten the ball end to bring the knot up to the needle.

Long-tail cast-on

This uses a single needle and produces an elastic knitted edge like a row of garter stitch.

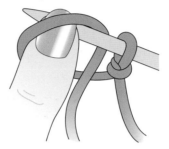 

1 Leaving an end about three times the length of the required cast-on, put a slipknot on the needle. Holding the yarn end in the left hand, take the left thumb under the yarn and upwards. Insert the needle in the loop just made on the thumb.

2 Use the ball end of the yarn to make a knit stitch, slipping the loop off the thumb. Pull the yarn end to close the stitch up to the needle. Continue making stitches in this way.

Cable cast-on

This method uses two needles, and produces a smooth, elastic edge.

   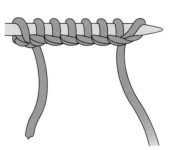

1 Make a slipknot with a short tail on one needle and hold this in your left hand (if you are right-handed). Insert the other needle as if to knit, wrap the yarn from the ball anticlockwise around the tip and pull the new stitch through the first loop.

2 Slip the new stitch onto the left needle in the direction shown. Two stitches are now on the left needle.

3 Now insert the right needle between the two previous stitches (not through the stitch loop), wrap the yarn as before and pull through to make another stitch.

4 Slip the new stitch onto the left needle as step 2. Repeat from step 3 as many times as required.

Knit stitch (k)

Choose to hold the yarn and needles in whichever way you feel most comfortable. To tension the yarn – that is, to keep it moving evenly – you will need to twist it through some fingers of the hand holding the yarn, and maybe even take it around your little finger. Continuous rows of knit stitch produce garter stitch.

1 Insert the right needle into the first stitch on the left needle. Make sure it goes from left to right into the front of the stitch.

2 Taking the yarn behind, bring it up and around the right needle.

3 Using the tip of the right needle, draw a loop of yarn through the stitch.

4 Slip the stitch off the left needle. There is now a new stitch on the right needle.

Purl stitch (p)

Hold the yarn and needles in the same way as for making a knit stitch. A purl stitch is the exact opposite of a knit stitch, producing a nubbly stitch to the front and a smooth V-like knit stitch on the opposite side. Alternate rows of knit and purl produce stocking stitch.

1 Insert the right needle into the first stitch on the left needle. Make sure it goes into the stitch from right to left.

2 Taking the yarn to the front, loop it around the right needle.

3 Lower the tip of the right needle, taking it away from you to draw a loop of yarn through the stitch.

4 Slip the stitch off the left needle. There is now a new stitch on the right needle.

Chain cast-off

A simple knit-stitch cast-off. Knit 2 stitches.* With the left needle, lift the first stitch over the second. Knit the next stitch. Repeat from * until one stitch remains. Break the yarn, take the end through this stitch and tighten.

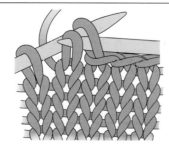

To cast off in pattern, simply work knit or purl stitches along the cast-off row as they would occur in the stitch pattern.

Slipping stitches

To slip a stitch is to pass it from one needle to the other without working into it. Various methods of decreasing (and many stitch patterns) require stitches to be slipped either knitwise or purlwise. The way you slip a stitch will affect the final appearance.

Slip one knitwise (sl1, Sl1, s1p, or S1p)

Slipping a stitch knitwise causes it to twist.

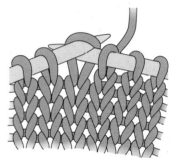

Insert the right needle into the stitch as if to knit it and slip it from the left needle onto the right.

Slip one purlwise (sl1p, Sl1p, or S1)

When a stitch is slipped purlwise, it remains untwisted.

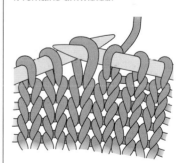

Insert the right needle into the stitch as if to purl it and slip it from the left needle onto the right.

Decreases

Decreases have two basic functions. They can be used to reduce the number of stitches in a row, as in armholes and necklines, and combined with increases, they can create stitch patterns.

Right-slanting single decrease (k2tog)

Knitting two stitches together makes a smooth shaping, with the second stitch lying on top of the first.

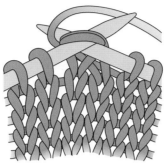

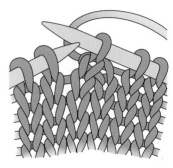

1 Insert the right needle through the front of the first two stitches on the left needle, then take the yarn around the needle.

2 Draw the loop through and drop the two stitches off the left needle.

Left-slanting single decrease (skpo)

Slipping a stitch, knitting a stitch, then lifting the slipped stitch over the knit stitch makes a decrease, with the first stitch lying on top of the second.

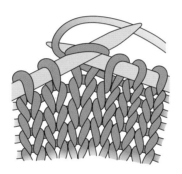

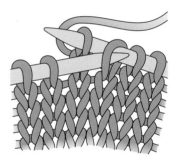

1 Insert the right needle knitwise through the front of the first stitch on the left needle, and slip it onto the right. Knit the next stitch.

2 Use the tip of the left needle to lift the slipped stitch over the knitted stitch and off the right needle.

Right-slanting purlwise decrease (p2tog)

This method is often used on the wrong side of stocking stitch to produce a stitch that slopes to the right on the right side of the work.

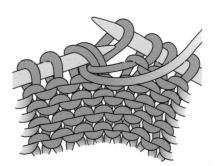

Insert the right needle purlwise through the first and second stitches. Wrap the yarn and purl both stitches together.

Left-slanting purlwise decrease (p2togtbl)
By purling stitches together through the back loops (tbl) on a wrong side row, this purlwise decrease forms a stitch that slopes to the left on the right side of the work.

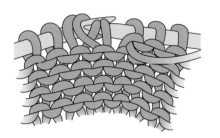

1 With the yarn at the front of the work, as when purling, turn the left needle towards you and insert the right needle through the back loops of the second and first stitches, from the back through to the front.

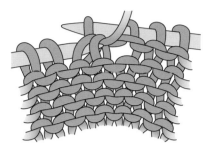

2 Wrap the yarn and purl both stitches together.

Balancing decreases

When shaping knitting, you can use the right- and left-slanting decreases (above) to create symmetrical sloping edges to your work, using either simple decreasing or full-fashioned decreasing:

Simple decreasing

This set-in sleeve head (below, left) is shaped in a curve, using simple decreasing at the edges of the knitting. The decreases on the right edge slope to the right, and those on the left slope to the left, creating smooth edges that can be neatly sewn in place.

Full-fashioned decreasing

This raglan sleeve head (below, right) is shaped with full-fashioned decreasing: left-sloping decreases on the right, and right-sloping decreases on the left, form lines that follow the shaped edges. You can work such decreasing at one, two or more stitches in from each edge, as desired (two stitches shown here). The front and back armholes of the garment would be worked with matching full-fashioned shaping to create an elegant design detail.

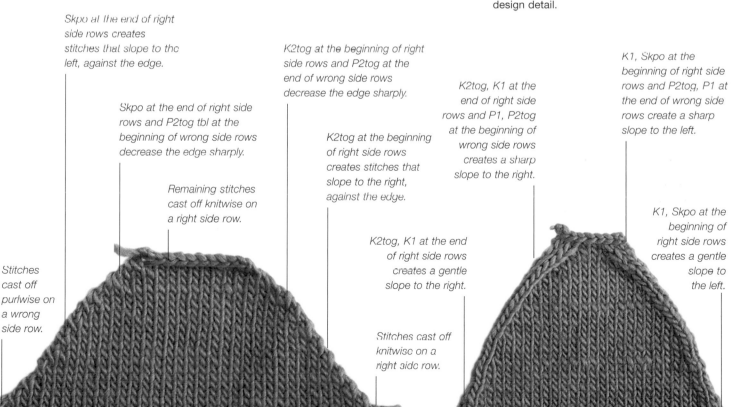

Skpo at the end of right side rows creates stitches that slope to the left, against the edge.

Skpo at the end of right side rows and P2tog tbl at the beginning of wrong side rows decrease the edge sharply.

Remaining stitches cast off knitwise on a right side row.

Stitches cast off purlwise on a wrong side row.

K2tog at the beginning of right side rows and P2tog at the end of wrong side rows decrease the edge sharply.

K2tog at the beginning of right side rows creates stitches that slope to the right, against the edge.

K2tog, K1 at the end of right side rows creates a gentle slope to the right.

Stitches cast off knitwise on a right side row.

K2tog, K1 at the end of right side rows and P1, P2tog at the beginning of wrong side rows creates a sharp slope to the right.

K1, Skpo at the beginning of right side rows and P2tog, P1 at the end of wrong side rows create a sharp slope to the left.

K1, Skpo at the beginning of right side rows creates a gentle slope to the left.

Increases

Here are three of the most basic methods of increasing a single stitch – yarn over, bar increase and lifted strand increase.

Yarn over (yo)

A yarn over makes an extra stitch with a hole at its base. It may be used either as a decorative increase or as part of a stitch pattern (when it will be balanced by a corresponding decrease). It's essential to take the yarn over the needle so that the strand lies in the same direction as the other stitches. Working into this strand on the next row makes a hole, but if the strand is twisted, the hole will close up. When the stitch before a yarn over is purl, the yarn will already be at the front, ready to go over the needle.

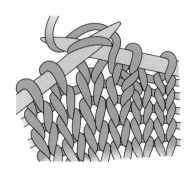

1 To make a yarn over between knit stitches, bring the yarn to the front as if to purl, then take it over the needle to knit the next stitch.

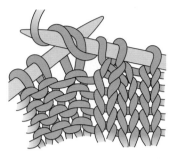

2 To make a yarn over between a knit and a purl, bring the yarn to the front as if to purl, take it over the needle and bring it to the front again, ready to purl.

Bar increase on a knit row (kfb)

Knitting into the front and the back of a stitch is the most common increase. It's a neat, firm increase, which makes a little bar on the right side of the work at the base of the new stitch. This makes it easy to count rows between shapings and doesn't leave a hole.

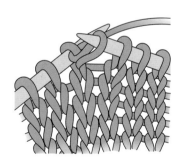

1 Knit into the front of the stitch and pull the loop through, but leave the stitch on the left needle.

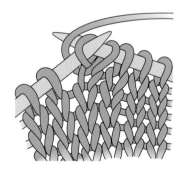

2 Knit into the back of the stitch on the left needle.

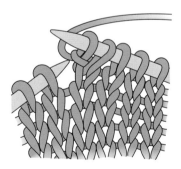

3 Slip the stitch off the left needle, making two stitches on the right needle. Note that the bar of the new stitch lies on the left.

Lifted strand increase to the left (m1 or m1L)

Making a stitch from the strand between stitches is a very neat way to increase.

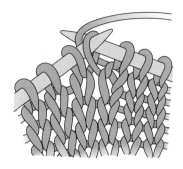

From the front, insert the left needle under the strand between stitches. Make sure the strand lies on the needle in the same direction as the other stitches, then knit into the back of it.

Lifted strand increase to the right (m1R)

This right-slanting increase balances exactly the lifted strand increase to the left.

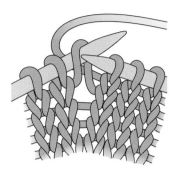

From the back, insert the left needle under the strand between the stitches. It will not lie in the same direction as the other stitches, so knit into the front of it.

Shaping with darts

Darts can be used to shape, for example, the waist of a sweater. Instead of decreasing and increasing at the side edges of the knitting, the shapings are arranged in a vertical line to form a decorative detail. The number of rows between the decreases and/or increases can be varied according to the angle of shaping required.

This dart is shaped with balanced decreases and increases, worked at either side of a single central stitch. Slip a split-ring marker onto the central stitch to help you work correctly, as shown. To decrease at the dart, work to 2 sts before the marked stitch, skpo, knit the central stitch, k2tog, work to end. These decreases are shown worked on every fourth row. Move the marker up as work proceeds. To increase at the dart, work to the marked stitch, m1R, knit the marked stitch, m1L, work to the end. Again, the increases shown here are worked on every fourth row.

Selvedge stitches (edge stitches)

Selvedge stitches may be added to the edges of a piece of knitting for various reasons: to stabilize an edge, to make sewing seams easier or to create a suitable edge for picking up stitches.

Garter stitch selvedge

Use this simple selvedge on stocking stitch, where edges will be joined into seams. The garter stitches make a firm edge, which can be neatly joined by working one stitch in from each edge when sewing the seam.

For a garter stitch selvedge at each edge, work every row as follows: K1, work as required to the last stitch, K1. This creates a vertical line of single garter stitches at each edge of the work.

Slip-stitch selvedge

This selvedge forms a line of chain loops, one chain for every two rows of knitting. This creates a lightweight edge with minimum bulk, useful where stitches will later be picked up, for example around a neck edge.

For a selvedge at each edge of the work:
Right side row: Sl1 knitwise, work as required to last st, K1.
Wrong side row: Sl1 purlwise, work as required to the last st, P1.

Chain stitch selvedge

This makes a neat edge for garter stitch, and is therefore useful when knitting ties, collars and other details where the edges of the work will be unattached. No further finishing is required.

For a selvedge at each edge of garter stitch, work every row as follows: With the yarn in front (as if to purl), slip the first stitch knitwise, take the yarn to the back between the needle tips, K to end.

Picking up stitches

Stitches may be picked up along one or more edges of a piece of knitting to create details such as collars and bands, eliminating the need for a bulky seam.

Hold the knitted piece with right side facing you. Insert the needle under one stitch at the edge, wrap the yarn around it and pull a loop through to make a stitch. Repeat as required.

As a rule, pick up one stitch from every row. This makes a neat, even join, but you may have too many stitches: if so, on the next row work several decreases, evenly spaced.

When picking up stitches from a cast-on or cast-off edge, pick up one stitch from every stitch along the edge, and adjust the total as above, if necessary.

Seams

Invisible seam

Sometimes called ladder stitch or mattress stitch. Place both pieces of knitting flat, with right sides facing and the edges to be joined running vertically. Thread a wool needle with yarn and secure at one lower edge – the first side. Take the needle under the cast-on edge of the second side, draw the yarn through, then go under the first cast-on edge again. Tension the yarn to level the edges. Take the needle under the strand between the edge stitch and the next stitch on the first row of the second side, and draw the yarn through. Repeat for the first row of the first side. Continue joining row ends from alternate sides in this way, without splitting stitches.

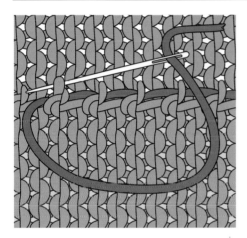

Slip stitch

Catching down pocket linings or zip facings is easy with slip stitch. With wrong sides facing, tack the pieces to be joined, matching rows. Thread a wool needle with yarn. Secure the end, then take the needle alternately under a strand on the main fabric and an edge strand. Don't let the stitches show on the right side or pull the yarn too tight.

Grafting

Grafting is used to join two rows of stitches that have not been cast off, and when worked correctly the seam is indistinguishable from a knitted row. Use a blunt-tipped yarn needle to avoid splitting the stitches.

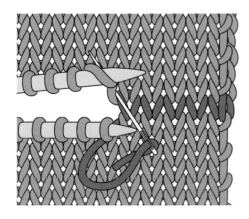

Thread a yarn needle (YN) with matching yarn (photo shows contrasting yarn, for clarity). Lay flat the two edges to be joined, right sides uppermost, and secure the yarn at upper right of the seam.
Pass YN knitwise through the first stitch on upper needle, and purlwise through the first stitch on lower needle.
* Pass YN purlwise through first stitch on upper needle, then knitwise through next stitch on same needle. Drop the first stitch off upper needle. (This step is shown in the illustration). Pass YN knitwise through first stitch on lower needle, then purlwise through next stitch on same needle. Drop the first stitch off lower needle. *
Repeat from * to * along the row, pulling each stitch gently to match the size of the knitted stitches. Secure the yarn tails on the wrong side of the work.

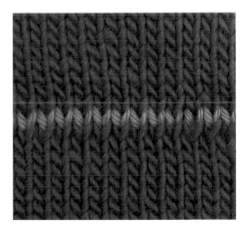

This completed graft looks exactly like a row of knitting, and will drape and stretch in the same way. Worked in matching yarn, the seam would be invisible.

Useful information and resources

When buying materials and equipment, you may come across items that have come from another continent, and it is always useful to know how to convert unfamiliar terms and lengths to those you are familiar with. Below are some charts to help with quick conversions. There is also a handy chart summarizing yarn categories and their corresponding tension and needle size, as well a list of Web resources.

Useful conversions

- Centimetres x 0.394 = inches
- Inches x 2.54 = centimetres
- Grammes x 0.035 = ounces
- Ounces x 28.6 = grammes
- Metres x 1.1 = yards
- Yards x 0.91 = metres

Equivalent weights

- ¾ oz = 20 g
- 1 oz = 28 g
- 1½ oz = 40 g
- 1¾ oz = 50 g
- 2 oz = 60 g
- 3½ oz = 100 g

Equivalent needle sizes

Choosing the correct size (diameter) of needles is crucial to obtaining correct tension (see page 18). Needles are sized in the US from 0 to about 20, and in Europe from 2mm to 15mm or more. There is not an exact match between the two systems. You can use needles sized by either system, provided you check your tension carefully.

US	EUROPE
0	2mm
1	2.25mm
2	2.75mm
3	3mm
4	3.25mm
5	3.5mm
6	4mm
7	4.5mm
8	5mm
9	5.5mm
10	6mm
10.5	6.5 or 7mm
11	8mm
13	9mm
15	10mm
17	12 or 13mm
20	15mm

Categories of yarn, tension ranges and recommended needle sizes

This chart was compiled by the Craft Yarn Council of America and reflects the most commonly used tension and needle sizes for specific yarn categories.

Type of yarns in category	Sock, fingering, baby (3-ply)	Sport, baby (4-ply)	DK, light worsted	Worsted, afghan, Aran	Chunky, craft, rug	Bulky, roving
Knit tension ranges in stocking stitch to 10cm (4in)	27–32 sts	23–26 sts	21–24 sts	16–20 sts	12–15 sts	6–11 sts
Recommended needle in metric size range	2.25–3.25mm	3.25–3.75mm	3.75–4.5mm	4.5–5.5mm	5.5–8mm	8mm and larger
Recommended needle US size range	1 to 3	3 to 5	5 to 7	7 to 9	9 to 11	11 and larger

Web resources
Below is a selection of some useful Web contacts for knitting suppliers, communities and guilds.

The Craft Yarn Council: www.craftyarncouncil.com
The Knitting Guild Association: www.tkga.com

Selected suppliers
www.buy-mail.co.uk
www.coatscrafts.co.uk
www.colourway.co.uk
www.coolwoolz.co.uk
www.designeryarns.uk.com
www.diamondyarn.com
www.ethknits.co.uk
www.e-yarn.com
www.hantex.co.uk
www.hook-n-needle.com
www.kangaroo.uk.com
www.karpstyles.ca
www.knitrowan.com
(features worldwide list of stockists of Rowan yarns)
www.knittersdream.com
www.knittingfever.com
www.knitwell.co.uk
www.letsknit.com
www.mcadirect.com
www.only-knitting.co.uk.
www.patternworks.com
www.patonsyarns.com
www.personalthreads.com
www.shetlandwoolbrokers.co.uk
www.sirdar.co.uk
www.spinningayarn.co.uk
www.theknittinggarden.com
www.upcountry.co.uk
www.vogueknitting.com
www.yarncompany.com
www.yarnexpressions.com
www.yarnmarket.com

Online knitting communities
www.ravelry.com
www.stitchnbitch.org

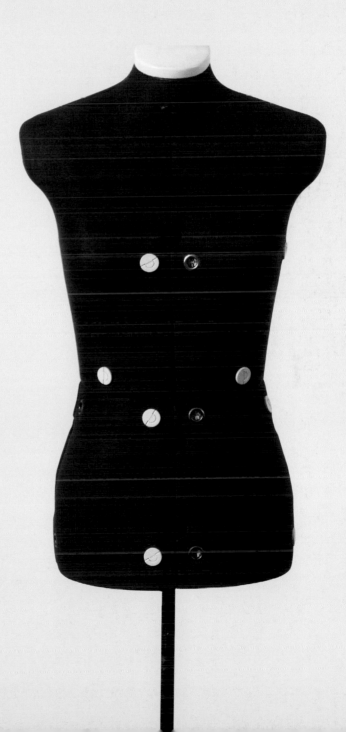

Glossary

3-ply, 4-ply: lightweight knitting yarns, sometimes called fingering.

Acrylic: a synthetic fibre.

Angora: very soft yarn fibre made from the combed fur of the Angora rabbit, usually blended with other fibres.

Aran-weight: a medium- to heavy-weight yarn.

Backstitch: a firm sewing stitch, also used to embroider fine lines and outlines.

Bamboo: fibre from the bamboo plant, used to make a smooth, silky yarn; also the woody stem, used to make knitting needles.

Batwing: a garment shape, normally with sleeves and body knitted all in one piece.

Block, blocking: treating a piece of knitting (by washing and/or pressing) to set its shape.

Bulky: a heavyweight yarn, sometimes called chunky.

Button band or button border: a separate band, knitted sideways or lengthways, to which buttons are sewn.

Buttonhole band or buttonhole border: a separate band, knitted sideways or lengthways, with buttonholes worked as knitting proceeds.

Cable: the crossing of two groups of stitches.

Cable needle: a small double-pointed needle used to work cables.

Casting off: fastening off stitches so they will not unravel.

Casting on: making new stitches on a needle.

Chain stitch: an embroidery stitch, used for medium-width, curved lines.

Chenille: a type of yarn that makes a velvety texture when knitted.

Chunky: a heavyweight yarn, sometimes called bulky.

Circular knitting: worked with a circular needle, or a set of double-pointed needles, to form a tube.

Cotton: a natural fibre from the cotton plant.

Counted-stitch embroidery: worked by stitching over knitted stitches, following a chart.

Crew (neck): a round, close-fitting neckline.

Cuff: the lower border of a sleeve.

Dart: a wedge of fabric 'pinched out' of a garment to allow shaping

Decreasing: working stitches together to reduce their number.

Double knitting: a medium-weight yarn.

Double-pointed needle: a knitting needle with a point at each end.

Drape: the feel of yarn or knitting, and how it behaves in use.

Dress form: a mannequin used to assist in the making up of garments.

Drop shoulder: formed by a sleeve with a straight-top edge, joined to a garment body with no armhole shapings.

Dye-lot number: indicates exact dye bath used, not just shade.

Ease: the difference between body measurement and actual garment measurement.

Felting: the process of shrinking knitting to make a firm fabric.

Fingering: a fine weight yarn (similar to 3-ply and 4-ply).

Flat seam: a method of joining knitted pieces.

Freestyle embroidery: worked by following a drawn or traced outline.

French knot: an embroidery stitch forming a small rounded knot.

Full fashioned shaping: shaping emphasized by working decreases (or increases) two or more stitches in from the edge of the work.

Garter stitch: formed by working all stitches as knit on every row.

Grafting: a seamless method of joining knitted pieces.

Hank: a coil of yarn.

Increasing: making extra stitches.

Invisible seam: a neat method of joining knitted pieces.

Knitwise: as when knitting a stitch.

Ladder stitch: another name for invisible seam.

Lazy daisy: another name for single chain stitch.

Linen: a natural fibre derived from the flax plant.

Lurex: a metallic fibre used to make yarn, either alone or blended with other fibres.

Mattress stitch: another name for invisible seam.

Metallic: yarn or fibre with a metallic effect.

Mohair: a natural fibre, hair from the Angora goat.

Natural fibre: fibre naturally occurring as an animal or vegetable product.

Needle gauge: a small gadget for checking the size of knitting needles.

Pattern: a stitch pattern, or a set of instructions for making a garment.

Picot: a little nub formed with knit or crochet stitches, normally repeated along an edging.

Polo neck: high, close-fitting collar that covers the neck.

Polyamide: a synthetic fibre.

Polyester: a synthetic fibre.

Purlwise: as when purling a stitch.

Raglan: a sleeve and armhole shaping that slopes from the armhole to the neck edge.

Ramie: fibre from the ramie plant, used to make a smooth yarn.

Reverse stocking stitch: stocking stitch worked with the purl side as the right side.

Rib stitches or ribbing: various combinations of knit and purl stitches, arranged to form vertical lines.

Ribbon yarn: a fancy yarn, made from flat tape.

Right and left (when describing parts of a garment): describe where the garment part will be when worn, eg, the right sleeve is worn on the right arm.

Right side: the side of the work that will be outside the garment when worn.

Ring marker: a smooth unbroken ring of metal or plastic, slipped onto a needle to mark a particular position along a row, and slipped from row to row as knitting proceeds.

Seam: the join made when two pieces of knitting are sewn together.

Seam allowance: the area between the sewing line and the edge of the cloth. You will need to add seam allowance to your patterns before sewing a toile.

Selvedge stitch: the first or last stitch(es) of a row worked in a different way to the rest of the row, to make a decorative edge, or a firm, neat edge for seaming.

Set-in sleeve: a sleeve and armhole shaping where the armhole is curved to take a curved sleeve head.

Shaping: increasing or decreasing the number of stitches to form the shape required.

Shawl (collar): a large collar that wraps the neck like a shawl.

Shetland wool: loosely spun sheepswool from the Shetland Islands.

Short-row shaping: the process of working incomplete rows to shape the knitting.

Silk: a natural fibre from the cocoon of the silkworm.

Single-chain stitch: an embroidery stitch used for flower petals, etc.

Single moss stitch: a stitch pattern with a dotted appearance.

Skein: a loosely wound coil of yarn or embroidery thread.

Slip stitch: a stitch slipped from one needle to the other without working into it. Also a sewing stitch used to produce a flat seam.

Slub yarn or slubby yarn: yarn of uneven thickness.

Sport-weight: a medium-weight yarn.

Stem stitch: a freestyle embroidery stitch.

Stitch holder: a device for holding stitches temporarily.

Stitch marker: a split ring of metal or plastic, slipped onto a knitted stitch to mark a position.

Stocking stitch: formed by working one row of knit stitches, one row of purl stitches, and repeating these two rows.

Swiss darning: an embroidery stitch that copies knitted stitches, also known as duplicate stitch or kitchener stitch.

Synthetic fibre: manufactured fibre, not naturally occurring.

Tacking: a temporary sewing stitch. Also known as basting.

Tapestry needle: another name for yarn needle.

Tension: the number of stitches and rows to a given measurement.

Toile: a prototype for a garment made in inexpensive fabric. Also known as a muslin.

Wool: a natural fibre from the coat of sheep.

Worsted: a medium-weight yarn.

Wrong side: the side of the work that will be inside the garment when worn.

Yarn needle: a sewing needle with a blunt tip and a large eye.

Yoke: the neck and shoulder area of a garment, especially where this is made all in one piece.

Index

Credits

Quarto would like to thank the following agency for supplying images for inclusion in this book:

Rex Features: Pages 13, 64, 72, 76, 88.

All other images are the copyright of Quarto Publishing plc. While every effort has been made to credit contributors, Quarto would like to apologize should there have been any omissions or errors – and would be pleased to make the appropriate correction for future editions of the book.

Authors' acknowledgements

Thank you to all who have supported us during the creation of this book, two legged and four. We would like to give special thanks to Adam, Joe, our families and Sibling: Cozette, Kate, Lucy, Alex, Hannah, Kiri. xxx